Empowering Our Children

...To Be More Effective in the Political Process

Empowering Our Children

...To Be More Effective in the Political Process

Salvatore C. Nicosia

Companion Press
P.O. Box 310
Shippensburg, PA 17257-0310
Internet: http://www.reapernet.com

Good Stewards of the
Manifold Grace of God

ISBN 1-56043-210-1

For Worldwide Distribution
Printed in the U.S.A.

Dedication

This book is dedicated to the very young children, and to those yet unborn, who will live most of their lives in the new millennium. They will need to be prepared for the many challenges they will certainly face during that time.

We are currently faced with a serious problem of trust in many of our leaders at all levels of government. Many of our leaders have succumbed to the lure of material gain and the attainment of power. We need to develop more leaders that will have a servant's heart and *serve* people, instead of *rule* them. Democracy needs to have citizens that are informed, effective communicators and active listeners, able to make intelligently formed decisions.

Alexis, Celeste, Jonathan, Heidi, and Kim: this book is for you. May it help you in your future years to be involved citizens of the great country we call the United States of America. Long may it live!!

Acknowledgments

This book is the result of many valuable contributions made by persons throughout my life: my parents who nurtured my life during my early years; my wife, Mary, who has tolerated my many shortcomings and has offered her timely words of wisdom to help, considerably, to smooth out my numerous rough spots; my children, Joseph and Joan, who helped give a purpose to life; my many teachers who taught me to think critically and encouraged me to ask questions as a part of the learning process; my students who keep challenging me to help them become all they are capable of becoming; and my colleagues, throughout the years, who offered their friendship and helped me to develop strategies to attain short and long range goals.

No man or woman is an island unto himself/herself. Each of us makes a difference either negatively or positively. I have had my share of meeting both negative and positive persons. I am thankful that I learned not to allow those of the negative mode to discourage me from working towards my goals in life, and that I was fortunate enough to meet more positive persons and to have the wisdom to follow their model of life.

More than ever, our children need positive role models they can look up to, helping to create hope for the future. I also want to acknowledge my grandchildren who will live most of their lives in the new millennium. Their coming into the world during the past few years helped motivate this endeavor.

Finally, I want to acknowledge the many persons in government who graciously wrote letters of recommendation that validated the need for this book. They include: Congressman Mike Forbes, First C.D., New York; State Assembly Women Patricia Acampora and Debbie Mazzarelli; State Senator Caesar Trunzo; Suffolk County Executive Robert Gaffney; Suffolk County Comptroller Joseph Caputo; New York State Supreme Court Judges Robert Doyle, William Underwood, and Peter F. Cohalan; Family Court Judge Gregory Blass; Suffolk County Planner Dr. Dewitt Davies (former student 1963-4); Suffolk County Legislators Joseph Caracappa, Brian X. Foley, and Michael Andre; Suffolk County Clerk, Edward P. Romaine, and Felix J. Grucci, Jr.; Brookhaven Town Supervisor, Stanley Allen; Brookhaven Town Clerk, Lynne C. Nowick; Smithtown Tax Receiver, Frank B. Falco; Mayor of Islandia Village, Catherine Romanelli; Library Director of Sachem Library, Raymond Fell; Superintendent of Patchogue Medford Schools, James Ruck; Superintendent of Schools, Sachem School District, Dr. John Cassese; Principal of Waverly Avenue Elementary School, Sachem District, and long-time colleague, Larry Pillegi; Teacher of English at Seneca Junior High School, Sachem District, and close friend, Kathleen Erhardt; Director of College Relations of Suffolk Community College, and former student, Sal Bellafiore; fellow counselor at Patchogue Medford Schools, Cleveland Johnson; V.P. of Government Relations, Mariga Communications Corporation, John Wehrenberg; Fire Commission Holbrook Fire Department, former Suffolk

County Legislator, and former Deputy Commissioner of Suffolk Police Department, John Juston; Director of Suffolk County Salvation Army Operations, and Assemblyman, Thomas Barraga, who represents my district in Albany.

Table of Contents

Preface

This book is a political primer designed to help young students to develop an astute awareness of how our political system works and to motivate our future voters to become an active part of the political process.

This hands-on approach will help inculcate in the students a strong desire to actively participate not only in the voting booth but in attending public meetings and encouraging them to actively participate in political campaigns as candidates and supporters of candidates.

A Rationale for Teaching Middle Schoolers to Become More Politically Astute

A democracy needs to have well educated and well-informed citizens who can exercise their thought processes to intelligently select viable and effective leaders. They should be even motivated to consider running for public office themselves or support the candidacy of an office seeker in an active manner. They should be able to understand how the political system, we live under, REALLY works! They should know how to get involved in political campaigns and know how to assist candidates seeking to get elected. There is more to democracy than voting on election day!

It would be logical to assume that our education system would have a well established curriculum and well-trained teachers available to prepare our young citizens to look forward to actively participate in the political process in an intelligent and active practice. During my 41 years as an educator, I have been acutely aware that far too many teachers lack adequate training on how our political system works.

Suffolk Board of Elections statistics indicate, sadly, that too many citizens are not using their right to vote and are not even registered to vote. Today, as this is written, fifty percent of our population that is eligible to vote has not even bothered to register. Even those who are registered fail to vote regularly in November.

We even have a term called an "off-year election" to denote a year when there are no presidential or gubernatorial elections. During so called "off-year" elections, less than 40 percent of those who are registered bother to vote in November. This means that on those years less than 25 percent of the eligible voters actually go to the voting booth to cast their vote. Three out of four eligible voters stay home, only to complain about their lot while failing to try to do something about it.

Too many political office-holders know this and this awareness may be a contributing factor to their own lack of response to the public at large. What this means is that political office-holders use registered voter enrollment lists to know whom to target during primary and regular elections. Mailings are usually sent only to registered voters of their party, leaving unregistered voters uninformed about issues and encouraging them to register to vote.

The question that begs to be asked is, "why do so many eligible voters choose to stay home on election day?" Many answers are offered. One answer that never seems to be given is, "too many of our citizens have never been properly trained to appreciate how the process works and how to play 'in the game of politics.' "

A football coach could hardly expect to develop a winning team if he didn't explain the rules of the game and practice game strategy. Yet we expect our young citizens to actively participate in the political arena without knowing how the "game" is played! A generation of teachers who lack political astuteness themselves is trying to educate our youth to become active in the political arena.

It is time to provide proper training for those who will teach our children effectively in this important area of their lives. This book is offered to be used for that purpose. It is time that our educational hierarchy examines where we are now and where we are heading. We owe this much to our children. As a grandfather of five children, I would like to leave them a legacy of remembering me as having tried to correct a serious shortcoming in our Social Studies curriculum.

Apathy caused previous democracies to fail. Let us move into the twenty-first century with viable political goals and teaching strategies that will augur well for those who will live in the blessed land during those hundred years!

As a Social Studies teacher, I learned many important lessons from the courses I took in training for that position, and from the years spent teaching our children. Those cultures that fail to correct their wayward ways are destined for the diminution of their status. Let us not let this happen to our nation!

November 1, 1996
Salvatore C. Nicosia
50 Pine Street
Holbrook, New York 11741
516-588-4693

Introduction

Since my college days, I have been actively involved in politics and government. I was fortunate in having had the opportunity to be in a Government class during my early years at City College New York. The date was 1948. One of my assignments from that class was to do an interview of a district captain from my election district. This person represents a political party (Democratic, Republican) and is ELECTED to his position by the REGISTERED voters of the party s(he) represents. (More about this person later.)

I decided to locate a Democratic district captain and ask if I could have an interview with him. I was not old enough to vote at the time because I was 20 years old and you had to be 21 years old to vote. I found it difficult to locate the Democratic district captain even though I went to the right place. I then went to the Republican assembly district leader, a hospitable, friendly, elderly man named Mr. McCabe.

He graciously gave me his time when I stated what I was looking for. He invited me to attend the next meeting of the district captains from his assembly district. I was introduced to a number of district captains from his assembly district and was very impressed by the friendliness displayed by those I met. I asked the assembly district leader to introduce me to my election district captain.

At this point, he asked me if I would like to BECOME a district captain of my election district. I responded with a reluctant "yes." I later discovered that the Republicans were outnumbered by an 8 to 1 ratio in that assembly district located in the Bushwick section of Brooklyn, New York. It was difficult to recruit district captains under those circumstances.

He explained my role as a district captain and this started my involvement in the political arena. This simple assignment turned out to be my passport to understanding the political system and how it works. It was a very practical study of the people who are involved in that process. Involvement in politics can be very exciting and rewarding!

I firmly believe that had I not had that experience, there is a strong possibility that I would not have learned how the political process REALLY works. Very little of my Social Studies courses in high school and college gave me a real understanding of the system as did my hands on experiences as a district captain and what ensued later.

After 41 years of teaching and counseling students, it is my strong belief that youngsters have an innate curiosity about events taking place immediately around them. Sadly, too many students leave school oblivious of important current political events and how they effect their lives. More importantly, they do not see that they could do something about those circumstances.

Well-trained, effective, and enthusiastic teachers can help children develop the necessary skills that will make them politically astute citizens. As we approach the 21st century, there is an urgent need to address ourselves to two very important issues:

1. Are our teachers being properly trained by our teacher training schools to be knowledgeable about how our political process REALLY works?

2. Are we going to continue to ignore the fact that fewer citizens are participating in that process?

There IS a viable solution. It needs to be set in motion ASAP. Our future citizens deserve to have that experience while in school. Our country's future depends on it!

Proposal

Middle school students have arrived at a stage in their mental development where their curiosity of what is going on in their immediate environment is starting to peak. At that stage, they are very teachable. With proper motivation and well-planned activities, long-lasting impressions can be achieved in their fertile minds!

During the past four years, I have been teaching students how to become more politically astute. Each week, on Tuesday mornings, I have met with students and presented them with the challenge of learning how the political process works. Field trips have been planned and taken to visit various government officials. Village, town and County government workers have been invited to speak to the class and interact with the students. The guest speakers have been spread out throughout the school year.

The response from the students has been very positive. Parents have commented that their children are reading newspapers more often and watching TV newscasts. Parents in our school have been very cooperative and have helped transport the students to the field trip location. Parental involvement has increased the success of this endeavor. Many parents have expressed that their own interest in the political process has increased because of their child's experience.

The cooperation from the government agencies has also been most encouraging. Materials relating to governmental functions has been readily available (at no cost). The two classroom teachers who have worked with me for the past four years have said they, too, have learned much about our political system since I started teaching their students. The teachers have not had any difficulty completing the (existing) required Social Studies curriculum.

The author feels strongly that extending this study over the sixth and seventh, or seventh and eighth grade will give the teacher an opportunity to schedule guest appearances and field trips over a two-year period. This provides the student with a gradual assimilation of the content involved in the study of village, town, school district, County government, as well as how the political system works in general. Extending the course of study over two years also provides the opportunity for the teacher to use the two November elections for political office, the two elections of school boards of education, etc., which take place during that time.

Students will learn how to interview political figures that visit the class and government officials they meet on field trips. A guest speaker can be invited during the first month of school, a field trip can be planned for the following month, and each ensuing month a guest speaker and field trip can be alternated. Thus in the 10-month school period, five guest speakers can address the class and five field trips can be planned for the class to go on. If the school has difficulties with field trip planning, they can increase the number of guest speaker invitations.

The sixth and seventh grade social studies curricula focus on geography and culture of the Asian countries and studies U.S. History from the age of exploration until the Civil War period. While it is important that children learn about their world and historical background, it is equally important for them to be politically astute, able to actively participate in the political process in their adult years. They should be able to vote intelligently, to participate at public meetings, and in political campaigns.

They may even run for political office and make a difference. In 1976, the author had the privilege of being nominated by the Republican party to run for U.S. Congress. It was an exciting experience! Although defeated by the incumbent, the political astuteness I learned during that campaign has been priceless.

GETTING OFF TO A GREAT START!

FORMAT: Schedule a Politically Astute Class weekly for a 45-minute period. Meet on the same day and same time.

1. Prepare a GLOSSARY OF POLITICAL TERMS that will be used frequently in discussions (suggested list enclosed).

2. WRITE a letter to the parents informing them of what their child will be experiencing during the school year. Include in your letter how they can help at home to make their children become more politically astute.

3. INVITE the parents to visit the scheduled weekly classes. It is important to get parents INVOLVED in this process. During the year, you will be asking parents to plan to take their children to schedule public meetings that will give their children a "HANDS-ON" experience that will greatly enhance the teacher's efforts in class.

4. During the first few lessons, focus on encouraging students to visualize what being a good citizen means to them. Discuss the term LEADER. Ask how does one become a Leader? List characteristics that best describes LEADERSHIP (please see attached list). Ask why it is important to choose good leaders and what kind of training is required to become a leader? Discuss who in their class they see as a leader and why they chose that person? Ask students to examine their own characteristics for leadership and prepare a list of characteristics they already have and characteristics they need to cultivate (develop). Students should begin to

realize that while some may find it easy to become leadership material, all have the POTENTIAL to develop into a leader!!

Note: Teacher should spend ample time on this important theme and review this issue later to learn how much was retained by the students. They need a great deal of reinforcement of this dynamic.

Once the teacher feels assured that the students have absorbed the concept of leadership (s)he can then begin to introduce the first lesson in government.

Leadership

In introducing the course, the class should be provided the opportunity to discuss what is LEADERSHIP? How are LEADERS chosen? What are the characteristics of leadership? Why is it important to select very effective leaders? Students should discuss leadership in their own class and how they would select a leader from their own class.

A listing of the characteristics of very effective leadership should be prepared and reviewed by class. They should use the prepared list (sampled below) to examine the leadership qualities of future guest speakers and political figures they meet in future field trips.

A VERY EFFECTIVE LEADER MUST BE:

1. A GOOD LISTENER.

2. Able to communicate ideas in an understanding way.

3. Hard-working.

4. HONEST and TRUTHFUL.

5. Helpful; enjoying helping others.

6. Knowledgeable about what is going on; aware.

7. A TEAM player.

8. PATIENT with others who may disagree with him/her.

9. Well-balanced, without taking himself/herself too seriously.

10. A good follower as well as a leader.

11. A person of integrity.

12. Visionary; able to see the consequences of decisions being made.

13. Energetic; willing to walk the extra mile.

14. Healthy (emotionally, physically, and psychologically).

15. Respectable; earning respect from those (s)he leads.

16. Responsible; taking his/her responsibilities seriously.

17. Encouraging; giving compliments to those (s)he leads, when appropriate.

18. A good role model to those (s)he leads.

SUGGESTED ACTIVITY FOR STUDENTS

As a means of impressing on young students the importance of registering to vote, the teacher can assign the following:

1. Show students how easy it is to fill out a voter registration form by having them complete one in class.

2. Give each student a voter registration form so they can visit their adjoining neighbors (with accompanying parent). The goal is to have a student locate a neighbor who is not registered and recruit that neighbor to register. When the student realizes that his/her own participation brought about the desired result, the student will gain from the exercise a true sense of involvement in the political process.

3. Led by the teacher, students should discuss what they experienced during their visits to their neighbors.

By fully participating in this exercise, students will develop a greater appreciation on the work done by elected committee persons in carrying out their responsibilities for their respective political party, and especially their efforts to get voters registered and encourage them to exercise their privilege to vote.

New York State Voter Registration Form

Vote New York

You Can Use This Form To:

- register to vote in New York State
- change you name and/or adress, if there is a change since you last voted
- enroll in a political party or change your enrollment

To Register You Must:

- be a U.S. citizen
- be 18 years old by December 31 of the year in which you file this form (*note*: you must be 18 years old by the date of the general, primary or other election in which you want to vote).
- live at your present address at least 30 days before an election
- not be in jail or on parole for a felony conviction
- not claim the right to vote elsewhere

Información en español: si le interesa obtener este formulario en espânol, llame al 1-800-367-8683

中文資料：如果你有興趣索取本中文資料表格，請電 1 - 800 - 367-8683

To Complete This Form:

Fill in all the boxes that apply to you.

Box 4: Give your home address

Box 5: Give your mailing address if it is different from your home address(post office box no., star route or rural route no., etc.)

Box 7: The completion of this box is optional.

Box 9: If you have never voted before, write "None." If you can't remember when you last voted, put a question mark(?). If you voted before under a different name, put down that name. If not, write "Same."

Box 10: Check one box only.

Box 11: This application must be signed and dated in ink.

If you will need an application for an Absentee Ballot or would like to be an Election Day Worker, please check below.

Please print or type in blue or black ink

Deadline Information:

You can register in person at your county board of elections on any business day, except election day. If you want to vote in an election, you must mail or deliver this form to your county board of elections no later than 25 days before the election in which you want to vote. Your eligibility to vote will be based on the date you file this form, and your county board will notify you of your eligibility.

Need More Registration Forms?

You can get registration forms at most state agency offices and post offices or at any county board of elections.

Questions?

Call your county board of elections. Find the phone number on the other side of this form. Or call 1-800-FOR-VOTE
Hearing impaired people with TDD may call 1-800-533-8683.

☐ Yes, I need an application for an Absentee Ballot

☐ Yes, I would like to be an Election Day Worker

1 Check boxes that apply:
☐ new registration and enrollment ☐ address change
☐ party enrollment change ☐ name change

2 Are you a U.S.citizen? ☐ Yes ☐ No
If you answered NO, do not complete this form.

For Board Use Only

3 Last Name | First Name | Middle Initial | Suffix

4 Address Where You Live (do not give P.O.address) | Apt. No. | City/Town/Village | Zip Code

5 Address Where You Get Your Mail (if different from above) | P.O.box, star rte.,etc. | Post Office | Zip Code

6 Date of Birth

7 Sex (Circle) M F

8 Home Tel. Number(optional)

9 The last year you voted | Your Address was (give house number, street, and city) | In county/state | Under the name (if different from your name now)

10 Choose a Party - Check one box only
☐ DEMOCRATIC
☐ REPUBLICAN
☐ CONSERVATIVE
☐ INDEPENDENCE
☐ LIBERAL
☐ RIGHT TO LIFE
☐ FREEDOM

PLEASE note: In order to vote in a primary election, you must be enrolled in a party.

☐ I do not wish to enroll in a party.

11 AFFIDAVIT: I swear or affirm that
- I am a citizen of the United States
- I will have lived in the county, city or village for at least 30 days before the election.
- This is my signature or mark on the line below.
- The above information is true. I understand that if it is not true I can be convicted and fined up to $5,000 and/or jailed for up to four years.

Signature or mark

X ____________________ Date

Please do not write in this space

I. THE FIVE LEVELS OF GOVERNMENT

A. VILLAGE (HAMLET, COMMUNITY)

B. TOWN

C. COUNTY

D. STATE

E. FEDERAL (NATIONAL)

Explain in some detail each level of government both from a geographical standpoint, and from a political viewpoint. For example, a village is a group of citizens living in a small geographic area that ELECT to establish their own SELF-GOVERNMENT. Point out that only some villages (communities) elect to govern their own civic affairs. A visit to a village hall to meet and interview the mayor and other elected officials will prove to be most beneficial to the class. A facilitative question to ask during the study of village government could be, "why do some citizens elect to have their own self-government at the village level, while others choose not to do so?"

Explain to class that the government was established to provide services, protection, and safety to the people it serves. Each level of government provides some similar services (example: roadbuilding). Some levels of government will provide services that the other levels cannot provide.

The federal government provides us protection with armed forces such as the Army, Navy, Marines, Coast Guard, Air Force, and Federal Bureau of Investigation. The state maintains a state guard and state police troopers. The County provides a police department to maintain law and order at the County level. Some towns provide a police department, as do some villages. The important thing to remember is that government helps, with the cooperation of its citizens, to provide the services needed to maintain a community's well being.

We will be studying the kinds of services provided by the different levels of government and how power is delegated to those officials ELECTED and APPOINTED to serve the people of our community at each level of government.

II. THE THREE BRANCHES OF GOVERNMENT

Help students recognize that there are three branches of government at EACH LEVEL of government. Introduce the term: CHECKS AND BALANCES. Use the dictionary to look up the definition. Have a discussion of this concept to develop an appreciation of why this concept of government is very important in a democracy. Define the term *democracy* (a way of life in which the people choose to govern themselves).

A. EXECUTIVE

1. Is responsible for carrying out the laws.

2. Provides protection and safety services in the community.

3. Enforces the law and apprehends (arrests) lawbreakers.

4. Prepares a budget for its services and works with legislative branch to spend the money properly.

B. LEGISLATIVE

1. Initiates (introduces) new laws called BILLS.

2. Passes the bills into law after long discussion of proposed legislation.

   a. Holds public hearings on proposed bills.

   b. Conducts debates on proposed bills.

3. Oversees how the laws are being enforced by the executive branch.

4. Approves the budget prepared by the executive branch and authorizes the money to be spent by the executive branch (appropriations).

5. Approves appointments made by the executive branch.

C. JUDICIAL

1. Interprets (explains) the laws so citizens can understand them.

2. Reviews cases brought before the court by a public attorney to determine if a trial should be held (referred to as an *indictment* procedure).

3. Tries persons accused of crimes (criminal) by jury trial or judge only.

4. Sentences those found guilty of crime to prison.

5. Hold trials to settle civil disputes between two citizens or groups of citizens.

SUFFOLK COUNTY ELECTED OFFICIALS

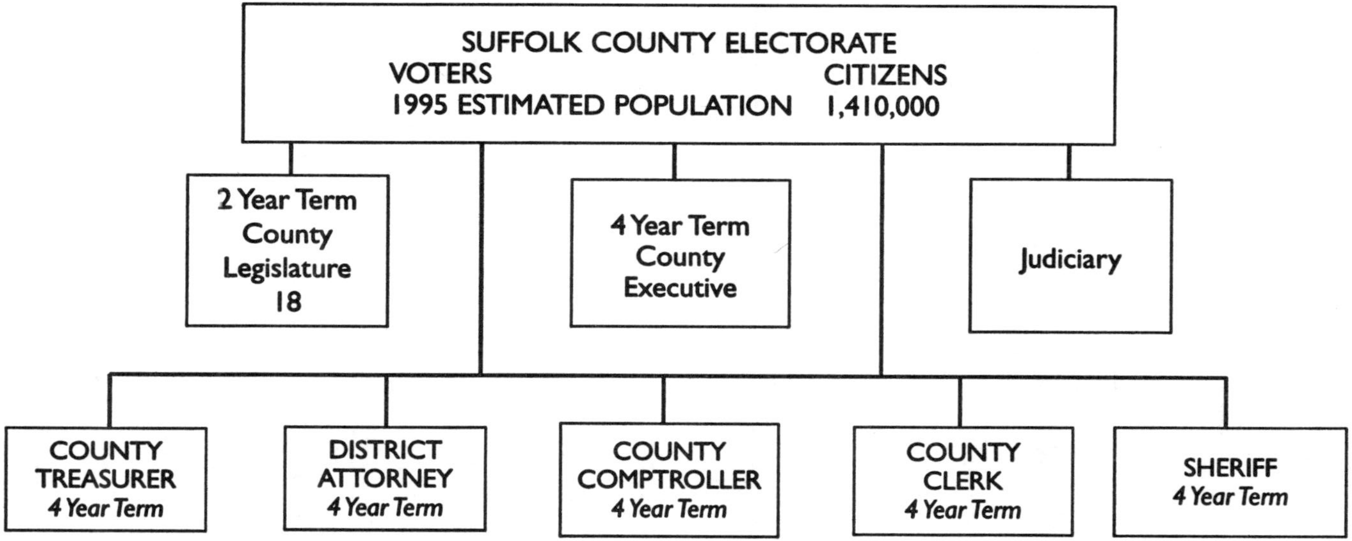

Elections held on odd years 1991 1993 1995 1997 etc.

INFORMATION SHEET OF ELECTED OFFICIALS FROM VARIOUS LEVELS OF GOVERNMENT:

My local area is: ______________________________

Fire District: My local fire commissioner is:

____

My school district is: ___________________________

School board members:
1. ____
2. ____
3. ____
4. ____
5. ____
6. ____

My election district is: __________________________

My committee members are:
1. ____
2. ____

Village Mayor (only in incorporated villages)

____

Village Board of Trustees (only in incorporated villages)

____
____
____

I Live in the Town of: __________________________

My Town Supervisor is: _________________________

____

My Town Board Members are:
1. ____
2. ____
3. ____
4. ____
5. ____
6. ____
7. ____

I live in the County of: ________________________

My County Executive is: ________________________

My County Legislator is: ________________________

I live in the state of: ________________________

My Governor is: ________________________

My State Assemblyman is: ________________________

My State Senator is: ________________________

I live in the United States of America.

My President is: ________________________

My U.S. Congressman is: ________________________

My U.S. Senators are:
1. ____
2. ____

Dear Parent:

Your child has now entered the sixth grade. It is an exciting time in his/her life. (S)he will become more inquisitive about the immediate environment and will begin asking many questions. This is all part of becoming a mature adult. I have scheduled a Political Astute class that will be scheduled regularly on Tuesday mornings from 8:45 A.M. to 9:30 A.M. The class is designed to help your child become more aware of how the political process works at the "grass roots" level. The dynamics of leadership are also to be discussed.

During the year, your child will be meeting people who serve important roles in government. They will learn how to interview these elected and appointed officials about the services they provide to the community. The class will also make field trips to visit a village mayor, town board, County legislature, board of elections and the County health department. They will observe the operations of these government offices and can ask questions and learn first hand about governmental operations. Guest appearances by a fire commissioner, County committee person, tax assessor, County legislator, and a town council member will also be part of their experiences.

Soon after you receive this letter, your child will be interviewing you about your political astuteness so that a viable debate can begin in the family circle. You are cordially invited to attend our weekly classes and observe this important process taking place. It is a privilege to have this opportunity to share this time with your child. We look forward to meeting with you during the school year.

Yours truly,

Salvatore C. Nicosia

SUGGESTED INTERVIEW QUESTIONS FOR STUDENTS TO ASK THEIR PARENTS:

1. In what political party are you registered?
2. Why did you register in that political party?
3. How many years have you been voting?
4. Have you voted in all elections? Primary, school district, fire district and general elections?
5. How do you feel about voting?
6. How do you choose who you are going to select as your candidate?
7. Did you ever think of running for political office?
8. Why do you think a candidate chooses to run for political office?
9. Why should I become more politically astute?
10. Do you know the names of your town committee persons?

This interview should take place during the early weeks of the school year. Class time should be allotted to have students read their parents' responses to questions and react to them in class.

Chapter One
LOCAL GOVERNMENTAL UNITS

Teachers should include a brief study of governmental units that are part of the local community. They include:

The Fire Commissioner and the Board of Fire Commissioners

1. Provide security against fires and encourage fire prevention.

2. Respond to any fires in forests, homes, businesses, stores, etc.

3. Conduct ongoing fire safety programs.

4. Inspect homes and other public buildings for fire hazards.

5. Train volunteer firepersons to handle equipment and how to deal with different kinds of fires (chemical, oil, pollutants, gases, etc.).

6. Prepare budget to purchase fire equipment (hoses, trucks, fire gear) and maintain fire stations.

7. Provide emergency medical services and ambulance service to hospital.

FIRE COMMISSIONERS are ELECTED to their important position in the community. He is an important official in the Community. He carries out important responsibilities. He should be invited to the class and interviewed by the class with prepared questions. Students need to be trained how to ask good questions much like media reporters. (please see enclosed list of questions).

Elections for fire commissioners are held annually and the voters are eligible to elect these officials of government. Unfortunately, very few participate in this important election. Our young students should be made aware that they should participate in ALL elections and select their community leaders wisely.

SUGGESTED QUESTIONS FOR STUDENTS TO ASK THE FIRE COMMISSIONER

Name of fire commissioner:

1. What is your responsibility as a fire commissioner?

2. Do you earn a salary?

3. How long have you been serving that office?

4. When did you start becoming interested in being a firefighter?

5. When did you start becoming interested in being a fire commissioner?

6. Why did you become interested?

7. Does your family worry about your safety?

8. Is your job full-time or part-time?

9. Do you get nervous when you receive a fire-alert signal?

10. Do you have to be a firefighter before becoming a fire commissioner?

11. How did you feel when someone died in a fire?

12. How do you feel about rescuing someone from a burning building?

13. How do you know when a person is ready to be a firefighter?

14. Why do you like your job?

15. Do you know everyone in the fire department personally?

16. Are there any changes you feel should be made in your fire department?

17. What is the morale of the firefighters?

18. Where and how do you train volunteer firefighter?

19. Why and when do most fires start?

20. Have any volunteer firefighters lost their lives?

21. How can I, as a citizen, prevent fires?

22. How well is fire equipment checked for safety?

23. Have you had any interesting experiences as a fire fighter?

24. Can you tell me about a tragic fire you experienced?

25. Have you received any citations or medals?

26. Have you ever been injured fighting a fire?

27. Is the fire equipment up-to-date?

The Organization of the School District

The local school district is a governmental organization that is funded by TAXES. A duly elected group is responsible for educating the children in the Community. The group that is ELECTED is called a SCHOOL BOARD. There can be as few as five members and as many as nine members on the Board. They are usually elected for a term of three years. There are some who are elected for five years. There is NO salary for the position but there is a great deal of POWER in the position that goes along with the responsibilities they are charged to carry out for the community. During the past 40 years there has been little or no interest shown by the citizens of the community as to how these elected officials carry out their important responsibilities.

The cost of educating our children has skyrocketed during the past 20 years and now more parents of the community are starting to increase their attendance at school board meetings and more are voting on school board and budget election days. These elections were held during different times of the year. One district, for example, could hold its election in May and another in June. A New York State Law, just passed in 1995, mandates that all school budget and board elections will now be held on the second Tuesday in May. In 1996, ALL school districts in New York State will hold their election on the same day!

Educating our children is costly. It costs an average of around $10,000 to educate each child in school every year. Taxes for schools are raised from property tax at the local level and state taxes at the state level.

In recent years, many school budgets have been defeated because district residents have felt that the cost of educating our children has become too costly. There has been much debate on this issue and this has caused opposing factions (groups) to develop in school districts. Stormy school board meetings result in hard feelings and deep resentments among the citizens in the community.

Sixth and seventh grade students are in the midst of their educational development. They are becoming aware that people are making decisions that affect their present and future lives. Students should be presented with opportunities on how the educational system works in their community. It is recommended that the students be given an opportunity to meet a school board member and have prepared questions to pose to the school board member when he meets with them on a planned visit to their class. The teacher can distribute a sheet with stimulating questions to help the student gain insights into some of the dynamics and complexities of an educational system.

These insights will help the student gain a deeper appreciation for his/her education and how (s)he can contribute to that important process. The teacher should emphasize that it is important not only to vote for school budgets and school board members but to consider attending meetings as often as possible, participate in getting good citizens to run for that important office, and to even consider being a candidate themselves!

Democracy cannot continue to be viable if the citizens become apathetic and leave government to a select few. Statistics sadly indicate that this is becoming a stark reality as more and more citizens fail to participate in the political process. As children become politically involved early in their lives, the author strongly feels that they will be more active politically in their later lives.

WHAT STUDENTS SHOULD KNOW ABOUT THE SCHOOL DISTRICT ORGANIZATION

School board members:

1. Are elected for a term of three years (some for five).
2. Receive NO SALARY.
3. Appoint a School Superintendent to administer the schools in the district.
4. Review and approve curricula (what students learn) .
5. Approve the hiring of ALL SCHOOL PERSONNEL:
    a. Teacher
    b. Cafeteria staff
    c. Secretarial and office staff
    d. Custodial and maintenance staff
    e. School security staff
6. Approve CONTRACTS for following EXPENDITURES:
    a. School bus transportation costs and purchase of school-owned buses.

b. Building new schools.

c. Repairing existing buildings.

d. School Equipment such as desks, furniture, etc.

e. Purchase of uniforms used by students in athletic events plus equipment used by students.

f. Purchase of school textbooks, library books, etc.

g. Purchase of school supplies for maintaining school operations, cleaning material (floor wax, soap, paper supplies, etc.).

h. Approve photographers who take student photos.

7. Approve school field trips.

8. Set school calendar.

It is strongly recommended that besides inviting a school board member to visit the students, a field trip to a school board meeting should be planned during the time the students are learning about the school district organization. Parents should be encouraged to attend the meeting with their child. This experience would greatly enhance what the teacher was trying to instill in the classroom lessons. Students should be given an assignment to write an essay about their impressions about their school district and how it is administered.

QUESTIONS FOR STUDENTS TO ASK A SCHOOL BOARD MEMBER DURING HIS/HER VISIT AS A GUEST SPEAKER

1. What made you decide to run for the position of school board member?

2. Is there a salary for the position?

3. What are your responsibilities as a member of the school board?

4. What is your philosophy of education?

5. Do you have children in school?

6. What problems do you deal with in your role as a member of the school board?

7. What is your term of office?

8. What should we as young students look for to understand how the school district operates?

9. How many people vote during an election for school board members and the school budget?

10. How many members are there on a school board?

11. Do you have differences of opinion during meetings?

12. How do you settle these differences?

13. Do you think our students are getting the best education?

14. What would you improve in helping students get a better education?

15. Are teachers sufficiently trained to educate today's generation of children?

16. What would you recommend to our class to become well-educated?

17. Do you have any difficulties in carrying out your responsibilities as a board member and earning a living for your family?

18. How much reading of material is involved being a school board member?

19. Do you help decide if a teacher receives tenure?

20. Do you think giving a teacher tenure is appropriate? Why? Why not?

The Community Library Organization

A small but significant unit of government in the community is the LIBRARY. The library carries out an important responsibility to the members of the community. The voters in the community ELECT a group of members called the LIBRARY BOARD OF TRUSTEES. The members are elected for a term of FIVE YEARS. They do not receive any SALARY. Meetings are held on a monthly basis.

The agenda of the meetings deals with expenditures to be paid such as staff salaries, repairs to keep the building well-maintained, and purchase of books that members of the community want to read. The trustees also approve salaries for the staff members who maintain the books and other media that is located in the library. They also appoint a library director who is responsible for administering the library staff members and keeping records of all activities in the library. Library trustees attend library conferences that are held on an annual basis to become better informed on their responsibilities to serve their community well.

Students should know the following about their community library:

1. The library director is the chief administrator of the library.

2. The board of trustees:

    a. Sets the policy of the library

    b. Approves salaries of staff members.

c. Approves improvements needed from time to time to keep library in proper order.

d. Approves all purchases made by the library personnel.

e. Approves the hiring of staff members.

f. Approves the calendar of the library.

g. Interviews candidates for library director and makes final selection.

h. Prepares the library budget which is presented annually to the voters for their approval. (Library budgets are RARELY DEFEATED.)

Teacher should arrange for visit of library director or trustee to class and have students ask questions about his/her responsibilities in the library. A suggestion for an essay question assignment would be, "the importance of the library in the community!"

QUESTIONS FOR STUDENTS TO ASK LIBRARY DIRECTOR ON CLASS VISIT

1. What are the qualifications for being a library director?

2. How much schooling is necessary to become a library director?

3. What are your responsibilities as a library director?

4. Are children reading more or less these days?

5. Why do you think so few people participate in library budget votes?

6. What are the qualifications a citizen needs to run for library trustee?

7. What do you do to encourage readers to visit the library?

8. What can I do to make better use of the library facilities?

9. What changes do you see taking place in the near future that will affect the community library?

10. How do you go about deciding which books to purchase for the community?

11. Can I attend a library board meeting?

12. What made you decide to follow a career in library science?

13. Is there a good future in library work?

14. What are the salaries a person can earn working in the library?

15. Would you recommend your position? Why?

The Village Government Organization

Students should become very acquainted with the ELECTED and APPOINTED officials of an INCORPORATED village (a self-governing community).

The Mayor

The chief executive of the village is the MAYOR. (S)he is ELECTED for a term of four years. She presides at meetings of the board of trustees scheduled on a monthly basis. (S)he APPOINTS persons to the following positions in village government:

1. Village clerk
2. The planning board members
3. The zoning board of appeals
4. The assessor
5. The historian
6. Attorney
7. Treasurer
8. Senior building inspector
9. Ordinance enforcement officer
10. Director of community development agency

11. Highway department foreman

12. Sanitation foreman

13. Superintendent of recreation and parks

These departments carry out services to the citizens living in the village. A typical INCORPORATED VILLAGE has a population of five to seven thousand citizens. Students should be able to grasp the concept that the services provided by these village officials are important to the well being of the citizens that are being served by them. As students begin to study the other levels of government, the student can readily see that the services provided in the village are also provided, on a larger scale, at the TOWN, COUNTY, STATE, AND FEDERAL Levels. ANNUAL REPORTS are prepared by the incorporated villages are available from the village clerk's office.

The mayor does not work FULL-TIME at his/her job. (S)he earns a salary of less than $5,000. As an elected official, (s)he is very visible in the community. The village mayor is a neighbor and very accessible.

The Village Board of Trustees

The VILLAGE BOARD OF TRUSTEES usually consists of five to seven members. The trustees are ELECTED for a term of TWO YEARS. This board proposes RESOLUTIONS (ORDINANCES, LAWS). The mayor PRESIDES over the meetings, which are usually held on a MONTHLY basis. A QUORUM of at least three present members is necessary to conduct a LEGAL meeting.

The general public must be officially informed by NEWSPAPER NOTICES well in advance of the planned board meeting. Citizens are permitted to speak at these meetings on what is on the AGENDA at designated time periods during the public meeting. Most PUBLIC MEETINGS are held in the evening which gives the citizens a better opportunity to attend.

Depending on the AGENDA, meetings usually last for a period of two hours. When the annual budget is discussed, BOARD MEETINGS can become very lengthy. This is due to the fact that the amount of money being APPROPRIATED (planned expenses for the coming year) effects what the TAX RATE will be for the next FISCAL (financial) year. Citizens usually are very concerned about how much taxes they are going to pay. Part of the price we pay for living in a DEMOCRACY (a form of government where the people rule or govern themselves) is to be patient and listen to ALL sides of the issue before making a wise decision.

Young people need to witness the deliberations that take place at public meetings. Unfortunately, these meetings can at times, be tedious and boring, but it is a necessary process that must be endured. The price of freedom is responsibility to become aware that if we deprive the other person of his rights to speak and express his opinions, we stand the chance to lose our own rights if others don't have the right attitude of listening to us as we express our views. At the GRASS ROOTS LEVEL teachers have a great opportunity to develop a foundation for teaching about other government levels.

The VILLAGE BOARD OF TRUSTEES, besides attending regularly scheduled board meetings to conduct

LEGISLATIVE MATTERS, are also assigned responsibilities that relate to EXECUTIVE MATTERS. The VILLAGE MAYOR as CHIEF EXECUTIVE has APPOINTMENT POWERS. As a result, the village mayor appoints board of trustees members to various executive positions.

For example, one board of trustees can be assigned to oversee the traffic and safety division. Others can be assigned to code enforcement, highway, recreation, fire department, etc. Some villages give the trustees titles of COMMISSIONER to carry out their assigned roles. The mayor also DESIGNATES (names) one of the trustees DEPUTY MAYOR, who takes the mayor's place in his/her absence. As you can see, the mayor has quite a large responsibility and power to make many important appointments of persons who serve the village!

Due to the small size of a village, the mayor and the trustee board members wear "TWO HATS" performing the function of both executive and legislative matters. The student should be made keenly aware that, as the size of the POLITICAL UNIT increases geographically and in population, this double function does not occur.

The Village Justice

The village justice carries out the responsibility of punishing those who *violate* (break the rules) the VILLAGE ORDINANCES. The VILLAGE ATTORNEY represents the village in LEGAL matters and PROSECUTES (tries lawbreakers).

The village justice spends most of his/her time hearing trials of traffic violations. As we close our study of village government, a review of the different services provided by the VILLAGE OFFICIALS should be conducted. A field trip should be planned to the village hall and students should have questions to ask the mayor about his role in village government.

The teacher should prepare a list of questions the students can ask during the interview with the director of village planning and the mayor. The students can then use the MODEL prepared by the teacher for preparing questions to ask government officials at future field trips planned by the teacher. It should not be assumed that students would know what to ask a government official about his duties and responsibilities (suggested questions follow on next page).

SUGGESTED QUESTIONS FOR STUDENTS TO ASK THE DIRECTOR OF VILLAGE PLANNING

1. What made you decide to become director of planning?

2. What are your responsibilities in this position?

3. What qualifications do you need to have to become eligible for the position?

4. Is there a good future in your position?

5. Would you recommend your position to others? Why?

6. Is your position full-time or part-time?

7. What are my responsibilities as a citizen to help you do your job well?

8. Why is it important to be politically astute?

9. Do you believe that citizens are becoming more environmentally sensitive?

10. What salary do you earn in your position?

11. Did you get your position by taking a civil service test, or by political appointment?

12. Are you active politically?

13. What do you find the most interesting in your job?

14. What educational courses would you recommend us to take to be able to become better citizens?

15. When did you know you were going to attend college?

16. How did you go about selecting the college you attended?

The teacher should prepare a list of questions the students can ask during the interview with the mayor. The students can then use the MODEL prepared by the teacher for preparing questions to ask government figures during future field trips planned by the teacher. It should not be assumed that students would know what to ask a government official about his/her duties and responsibilities.

SUGGESTED QUESTIONS FOR THE STUDENT TO ASK DURING THE VILLAGE MAYOR INTERVIEW

1. What are some of your responsibilities as mayor?

2. Do you earn a salary?

3. How long have you been serving that office?

4. When did you become interested in being a politician?

5. Is the job full-time or part-time?

6. Do you like your job? Why?

7. What would you recommend for students to do to be prepared to get involved in government?

8. Why is it important to get prepared for our role as citizens?

9. Have you had any interesting experiences as mayor?

10. How do you select your staff members?

11. What are some of your goals for the village?

12. How does your role as mayor effect your family life?

13. What qualifications do you need to do to become mayor of a village?

14. Have you experienced any disappointments as mayor?

15. Would you recommend your job? Why?

16. What would I have to do to get involved in the village government?

17. How do you prepare a campaign to run for mayor?

18. Does it cost a lot of money to get elected mayor?

19. How do you raise money to run for office?

20. Are you running for re-election? Why?

Chapter 2
TOWN GOVERNMENT

Before we begin to develop an outline of the town government organization, let us first try to explain how the POLITICAL PARTY is STRUCTURED.

The Town Leader

The student should be introduced to a person called a TOWN LEADER. This person plays an important part in the POLITICAL PROCESS of town government.

How does (s)he get his/her position? To whom is (s)he responsible? The town leader is ELECTED by a group consisting of TOWN COMMITTEE PERSONS. The town committee person is ELECTED by VOTERS who are REGISTERED in the same POLITICAL PARTY in a political division called an ELECTION DISTRICT. The town committee person is elected for a term of TWO years. There are TWO elected town committee persons in each election district.

The town leader is elected by the town committee persons from ALL the election districts located in the TOWN.

Election of town leaders as well as town committee persons are held every two years.

NOTE: ELECTION FOR TOWN AND COUNTY OFFICE HOLDERS IS HELD ON ODD NUMBERED YEARS.

The town leader is responsible for PLANNING and carrying out the POLITICAL CAMPAIGNS that take place ANNUALLY. (S)he assigns key people in the political party:

1. To prepare campaign literature voters will read about the candidate.

2. To run fund-raising programs to pay for expenses to run a campaign.

3. To produce radio and TV commercials that help candidates to gain name recognition in voters' minds and what the issues of the campaign are.

4. To plan speaking engagements for candidates to give them widest exposure during the campaign period.

5. To motivate town committee people to distribute literature in their election districts and speak to voters in their district about the candidates running for office.

6. To help select candidates by appointing a screening committee who interview potential candidates in the party that want to be considered as the party nominee.

7. To organize the town committee into zones and choose zone leaders to keep tabs on how involved the various

town committee persons are in their respective jobs in their election district.

8. To distribute at a certain time of the year, usually late June, designating petitions to the town committee persons to circulate in their respective election districts to help get voter signatures that are necessary to qualify party nominees on the November ballot.

9. To conduct periodic town committee meetings to help keep party workers informed of what is happening in the political arena and to hear what is on the minds of the party membership.

10. To recommend office staff needed to operate the town committee business throughout the year.

11. To recommend to the town committee the executive officers that will assist him to administrate the town political organization. They include a vice president, secretary, and treasurer. These officers are elected by the members of the town committee organization. They are all elected for a term of two years.

The town leader has many responsibilities and wields a lot of AUTHORITY and POWER. (S)he needs to understand people well and exercise power and authority in a PRUDENT (wise) manner. History shows that many political leaders have exercised their power in a ruthless, selfish manner.

I would like to now point out why this has happened so often in the past and why it is necessary to teach our young citizens how the system works to that they can diminish the sometimes autocratic posture that town and other political leaders take in carrying out their important role in the political process. Hopefully, this political primer will pave the way for this to happen throughout our nation.

Young citizens need to know how our political leaders gain their positions, and how to keep them in check. This requires that TEACHERS develop an in-depth understanding of how the system works and that our SOCIAL STUDIES CURRICULA be examined carefully by those who can makes changes and re-prioritize the material we teach our children while they are attending our schools.

We should explore and review what has been happening during the past quarter-century in terms of how many of our citizens have lost their interest in participating in the political arena, and how cynical and mistrusting they have become. Well-informed, involved citizens are a strong safeguard against people who arrogantly seek positions of power and rule. These power-hungry people have learned that keeping citizens in ignorance assures them the opportunity to continue to be in power.

We owe our children the benefit of being PROPERLY TRAINED and to assume their participation in the POLITICAL PROCESS in an intelligent and meaningful manner.

Our universities and colleges need to add a POLITICAL PRIMER to their current courses of study, one that prepares future educators to teach children in the proper manner, leaving no room for doubt that the children will be readied for their future in the political arena.

It is the author's opinion, after having served in various governmental positions (such as library trustee, deputy commissioner of consumer affairs, candidate for U.S. Congress and County legislature, Suffolk County child protection committee member, Congressional aide, president of the local teacher association and delegate to various state and national conventions), that too many teachers lack adequate understanding of the "NUTS AND BOLTS" of the political process.

We can no longer afford the price we are paying in producing citizens that get "turned off" by what they hear about what goes on in politics. Our country's future is worth the investment of time, energy, initiative, and resourcefulness that need to be put into this worthwhile endeavor.

Let us now explore what responsibilities the TOWN COMMITTEE PERSON carries out for the people in his/her ELECTION DISTRICT.

The Town Committee Person

Let us begin by first asking, "how can an interested voter become a town committee person?" To be eligible, you must be a registered voter in a particular POLITICAL PARTY (Republican, Democratic). If you are eligible, you must know that the responsibilities of a town committee person are:

1. Helping potential candidates to get exposure in the election district by introducing the potential candidates to the voters in his/her district.

2. Attending political party meetings held on a monthly basis in POLITICAL CLUBHOUSES. In these club houses, meetings are held for the purpose of giving potential candidates and party nominees an opportunity to express their views on political issues, and getting suggestions about how to improve their candidacy for political office. Meetings are held all year round, and much socializing takes place in these clubhouses, helping to foster a camaraderie among the club members. Many club members are committee persons and much of the conversation during meetings is political in nature.

   Fund-raising events are held throughout the year for the purpose of paying expenses incurred in running the clubhouse. Officers are elected to conduct meetings and give them experiences in leadership roles. Town leaders attend periodic meetings to stay in touch with the members who help in campaign activities. Political clubhouses are "BREEDING GROUNDS" for future political candidates.

3. Helping elect the town leader, whose term of office is TWO years.

4. Attending meetings called by the town leader, usually every three to four months. Meetings held during the early Fall are most important, because by then election day COUNTDOWN has begun, and political activity becomes more intensive.

5. Circulating a DESIGNATING PETITION to VOTERS in the election district. Teachers should now view copy of designating petition and review with students. This

designating petition contains the name(s) of candidate(s) nominated by the political party during the political convention, held in late May or early June, when the process of selecting the candidates is completed.

These CONVENTIONS are often what is called a "GOING THROUGH THE MOTIONS" exercise. The designated party nominees are usually chosen by a SELECT EXECUTIVE COMMITTEE of the HIERARCHY of the party (that includes the district leader and officers).

A town committee person is usually given a designating petition that contains room for 20 voters to place their names, addresses, and the election district in which they reside. This task can usually be accomplished in two hours. The reason for the designating petition is to acquire the minimum number of signatures required, by New York State Election Law, for the party nominee to get on the NOVEMBER BALLOT.

The number of signatures for each candidate is determined by the office (s)he is seeking. A candidate for a town office, such as town supervisor or town council board member, may need 1000 signatures. A candidate for County executive might need 2500 signatures. A candidate for Congress might need 2000 signatures, and so on.

A book on this subject is published by the New York State Board of Elections in Albany, New York, and can be purchased for five dollars. It is worth the investment for every teacher planning to teach young citizens to be more POLITICALLY ASTUTE.

6. Inviting a candidate to WALK THE DISTRICT. (S)he takes the candidate to the homes of voters in the district to be introduced to the registered voters.

7. Planning neighborhood meetings and inviting the voters to attend and have candidates speak to them and answer the questions about the issues and how (s)he plans to address them when elected.

8. Distributing campaign literature during the final days of the election campaign. Voters need to feel that their committee person is representing their interests in the political organizations. This door-to-door effort is accordingly well received by the registered voters of the election district.

9. Making voters in their district aware of his/her desire to serve their civic (political) needs and to indicate how s(he) can be of service. (S)he prepares a business card (name, address, phone number) and distributes the cards to the voters in his/her district.

10. Spending election day making phone calls urging voters to go to the polls and vote.

11. Going to the polling places on election night, writing down the numbers read off the election machines. (S)he then calls in the tallied numbers to the town headquarters.

The tension during this period is high: this is the "MOMENT OF TRUTH" when the town committee person finds out how his/her district voted, and whether the work (s)he put into the campaign has resulted in VICTORY OR DEFEAT FOR THE CANDIDATES for which (s)he campaigned.

The town committee person can play a vital role in the political process. If made aware of his/her vital role and exercising it accordingly, (s)he can further the cause of democracy in the community, and restore confidence in our political system.

NOTE FOR TEACHERS: It is important for the students to develop a more than passing acquaintance with this important position. It is strongly suggested that teachers invite a town committee person to class to speak to students about what a town committee person does. Teachers should assist the students to prepare questions to ask the town committee person, further reinforcing what has been already taught by the teacher in previous lessons.

Students should be assigned to find out what ELECTION DISTRICT they reside in, and who represents them there. The cooperation of parents should be sought to help the student in his endeavor. Parents should be invited to attend your weekly class to help reinforce your work with your class. Suggest to students to try to meet their town committee persons.

Primary Election: What Is It? Why Is It Important?

Once the students have learned about the roles of the town leader and the town committee person in the political process, it would be of great benefit to the students to start explaining what a primary election is, and why it is important in the political process.

Suggested questions to pose in introducing this topic include: "What is a primary election? Why is it important

As Of March 31, 1995

ENROLLMENT LIST

1995

SUFFOLK COUNTY BOARD OF ELECTIONS

YAPHANK, NY 11980

BROOKHAVEN ED 214

U.S. CONGRESSIONAL DISTRICT #: 1
STATE SENATORIAL DISTRICT #: 3
STATE ASSEMBLY DISTRICT #: 3
COUNTY LEGISLATIVE DISTRICT #: 7

Gerald Edelstein
GERALD EDELSTEIN
Commissioner of Elections

Gerald Berger
GERALD BERGER
Commissioner of Elections

SUFFOLK COUNTY BOARD OF ELECTIONS
ENROLLMENT LIST

TOWN OF BROOKHAVEN ED#: 214

PAGE: 2
AS OF MARCH 31, 1995

NAME	PTY	RESIDENCE ADDRESS	MAILING ADDRESS
BENIGNO, ANTHONY M	B	15 CHERYL LN. PATCHOGUE 11772	
BENIGNO, BENEDETTO	D	15 CHERYL LN. PATCHOGUE 11772	
BENIGNO, DOROTHEA A	B	15 CHERYL LN. PATCHOGUE 11772	
DE MARCO, LAWRENCE W	B	16 CHERYL LN. N PATCHOGUE 11772	
DE MARCO, LESLIE	B	16 CHERYL LN. N PATCHOGUE 11772	
D' ANGELO, JOSEPHINE	R	19 CHERYL LN. PATCHOGUE 11772	
D' ANGELO, SALVATORE	R	19 CHERYL LN. PATCHOGUE 11772	
FLYNN, SUZANNE M	D	21 CHERYL LN. PATCHOGUE 11772	
PEPE, ANTHONY	R	1 DEBBIE LN, PATCHOGUE 11772	
PEPE, PAULA	R	1 DEBBIE LN. PATCHOGUE 11772	
SOUTER, RAYMOND E	B	2 DEBBIE LN. PATCHOGUE 11772	
SOUTER, ROSALIE	D	2 DEBBIE LN. PATCHOGUE 11772	
ZITTEL, ELEANOR M	R	3 DEBBIE LN. PATCHOGUE 11772	
COFONE JR, DANIEL A	R	7 DEBBIE LN. N PATCHOGUE 11772	PO BOX 388, MEDFORD NY 11763
COFONE, TARA J	B	7 DEBBIE LN. N PATCHOGUE 11772	PO BOX 388, MEDFORD NY 11763
BROWN, RUTH A	R	10 DEBBIE LN. N PATCHOGUE 11772	
TERRY, DAVID C	B	11 DEBBIE LN. PATCHOGUE 11772	
TERRY, RAYMOND W	R	11 DEBBIE LN. PATCHOGUE 11772	
TERRY, SHARON	R	11 DEBBIE LN. PATCHOGUE 11772	
HANSEN, KRISTINE L	R	12 DEBBIE LN. PATCHOGUE 11772	
HANSEN, MARIANNE	B	12 DEBBIE LN. E PATCHOGUE 11772	
HANSEN JR, PETER C	R	12 DEBBIE LN. PATCHOGUE 11772	
LOUGHLIN, FLORETTE B	R	14 DEBBIE LN. PATCHOGUE 11772	
LOUGHLIN, ROBERT E	R	14 DEBBIE LN. PATCHOGUE 11772	
MARCELLO, KEITH R	R	15 DEBBIE LN. PATCHOGUE 11772	
MARCELLO, MARGARET R	R	15 DEBBIE LN. PATCHOGUE 11772	
MARCELLO, VALENTINE R	R	15 DEBBIE LN. PATCHOGUE 11772	
SUDMANN, ANN-MARIE	D	16 DEBBIE LN. N PATCHOGUE 11772	
SUDMANN, CONRAD H	B	16 DEBBIE LN. N PATCHOGUE 11772	
HEWITT, ANTONINO G	R	17 DEBBIE LN. PATCHOGUE 11772	
HEWITT, TERESA	R	17 DEBBIE LN. N PATCHOGUE 11772	
HEWITT, TERRENCE	R	17 DEBBIE LN. N PATCHOGUE 11772	
JUDGE, MARY A	C	19 DEBBIE LN. PATCHOGUE 11772	
ALBERS, JOHN H	R	20 DEBBIE LN. N PATCHOGUE 11772	
BRIDESON, CAMILLE A	R	21 DEBBIE LN. PATCHOGUE 11772	
BRIDESON, LISA A	R	21 DEBBIE LN. PATCHOGUE 11772	
BRIDESON, PETER J	R	21 DEBBIE LN. PATCHOGUE 11772	
BRIDESON SR, ROBERT M	B	21 DEBBIE LN. PATCHOGUE 11772	
VITALE, GENOVEFFA	R	23 DEBBIE LN. PATCHOGUE 11772	
VITALE, GRACE	R	23 DEBBIE LN. PATCHOGUE 11772	
OSTRICK, CATHLEEN A	B	25 DEBBIE LN. PATCHOGUE 11772	
IMMEL III, MARTIN S	R	26 DEBBIE LN. PATCHOGUE 11772	
IMMEL, MARTIN S	R	26 DEBBIE LN. PATCHOGUE 11772	
IMMEL, MARY LOU	B	26 DEBBIE LN. PATCHOGUE 11772	
IMMEL, MICHAEL S	R	26 DEBBIE LN. PATCHOGUE 11772	
PORTELLO, TODD B	D	27 DEBBIE LN. PATCHOGUE 11772	
KEARY, JOHN P	R	29 DEBBIE LN. PATCHOGUE 11772	
KEARY, LISA A	R	29 DEBBIE LN. PATCHOGUE 11772	
ELSINGER, DIANA D	R	34 DEBBIE LN. N PATCHOGUE 11772	
ELSINGER, ROBERT F	D	34 DEBBIE LN. N PATCHOGUE 11772	
LICARI, BARBARA J	R	36 DEBBIE LN. N PATCHOGUE 11772	
LICARI, JOSEPH	D	36 DEBBIE LN. N PATCHOGUE 11772	
KROLL, JAMES M	R	38 DEBBIE LN. PATCHOGUE 11772	
KROLL, SUE E	R	38 DEBBIE LN. PATCHOGUE 11772	
MESSINA, DENISE M	D	1 GALE LN. PATCHOGUE 11772	

SUFFOLK COUNTY BOARD OF ELECTIONS
ENROLLMENT LIST

PAGE: 11
AS OF MARCH 31, 1995

PTY	PARTY NAME	TOTAL
D	Democratic	162
R	Republican	217
C	Conservative	15
L	Liberal	3
T	Right To Life	3
B	Blanks	135
	ED TOTAL	535

TOWN OF BROOKHAVEN
ELECTION DISTRICT NO. 214
Suffolk County Board of Elections

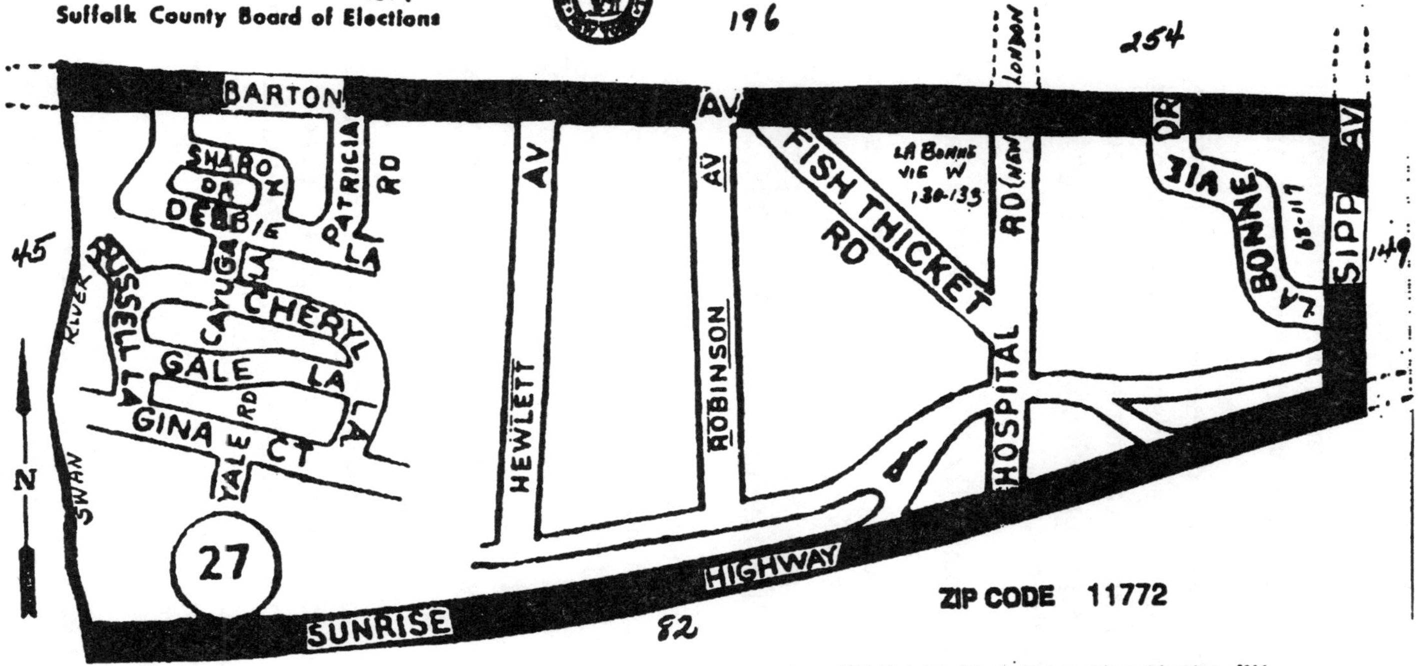

October 1980 District #82 divided to create District #214

'90

for voters to participate in them? Why do so few voters bother to vote on primary day? What do you think needs to be done to get more voters to vote on primary day?"

Before starting to answer these questions, it is important to remind the students that the town leader (who must also be a town committee person) is elected by the town committee person, who, in turn, is elected by the voters in the election district.

At this point, the teacher should explain that the town committee person is elected to his position on primary election day, held in September. The Republican committee persons are voted for during ODD number years, (1995, 1997, 1999, etc.), and Democratic committee persons are voted for during EVEN number years (1996, 1998, 2000).

The teacher can discuss with students that primary elections are not always welcomed by town and County political leaders. Some may even try to discourage primary elections. The reason for this is that a town or County political leader has the power to designate someone to be a town and County committee person if there are vacancies in any election district.

This means that if an election district does not have a registered voter of a particular party (Republican, Democratic, Independent, etc.) interested in running for that position on primary day, the town leader and County leader can fill that vacancy with the person of his/her choice.

It is very important for students to grasp that this is the root of one of our more serious problems in the political process. These appointments made by town and County leaders assures him/her of having strong control about who can run for political office. The chosen candidates are then under some political obligation to the town and County leaders. This sad state of affairs now exists on Long Island.

Young citizens must be properly trained to know what really is happening in their government, so they can take proper steps when they become eligible to vote and actively participate in the political process!

Today, too many committee persons have selfishly motivated agendas as reason for being committee persons. Many are APPOINTED positions in government, keeping them LOYAL to the political leaders. This is called PATRONAGE. It creates situations that cause voters to become disenchanted and discouraged, turning them off from voting.

That is why we have to train our children to understand the process! It is difficult to comprehend how an intelligent citizenry can allow such a flagrant abuse of policy to continue for so long. Patronage, although diminished, is still in operation. Children, properly trained in the political process, can greatly contribute to the eradication of "political bossism!" We need leaders, not bosses!

The Primary Election

A primary election is one of the least understood processes of our political system. Ironically, it provides the voter the opportunity to participate in a very important activity which is fundamental to our democratic way of governing ourselves. Why do so many citizens neglect to participate in a primary election? Does the average citizen understand how a primary works?

Statistics strongly indicate that our citizens have not been properly educated to understand this electoral process. When a person is not properly educated, his ignorance tends to inhibit him to participate in that process. When asked why they don't participate in the primary elections, many voters answer that it isn't important enough for them to bother or that it is none of their business.

Party leaders find primaries threatening because it divides the party "faithful" into different factions. At the annual convention held to nominate candidates, there may be a difference of opinion among the committee persons as to who the candidates should be (those seeking designating petitions to be signed by voters in their election district).

Any potential nominee who thinks s(he) should have been designated at the convention can challenge the party nominee and seek to get signatures from votes registered in that party. If a disenchanted party member decides to challenge the party nominee, s(he) sets in motion the following scenario (listed in a MANUAL published by the state board of elections):

1. Committee persons are approached by the disenchanted party member to assist him/her in seeking signatures necessary to get on the ballot.

2. Much “wheeling and dealing” takes place behind the scenes to try to persuade the disenchanted party member to have a change of heart.

3. A number of CAUCUSES are held to develop strategy to show solidarity among the party regulars.

4. Phone calls are made to committee persons to assess who is going to help the disenchanted party member.

5. Newspaper articles begin to publish stories that the political leader may be losing his grip of party reins.

6. Political leaders (COUNTY AND TOWN) have their work cut out for them to prepare a campaign to get their party designated nominees elected in September, when the primary election takes place.

7. The political clubhouses invite the candidates to speak at their monthly meetings during the campaign. The atmosphere in the clubhouses is strained because of the existence of divided loyalties at the meeting.

8. When designating petitions are submitted to the County board of elections by the disenchanted party member, the political leader assigns some workers to review the petitions to ascertain if there are any discrepancies in the petition that would void it.

   This is a very stressful period for a party member seeking to challenge a party nominee. The party member has unwittingly challenged the party leadership and his supporters and a strained relational situation ensues.

Often this results in long-lasting feuds that need not occur if mature heads were to prevail.

9. A final attempt is made by the political leaders to bring the disenchanted party member to court to try to legally get him off the ballot. They are occasionally successful because some disenchanted party members do not check their designating petitions (and dot every "i" and cross every "t"). There are many pitfalls to be aware of, when trying to challenge a party nominee.

10. Another phenomenon to be aware of is the role of the commissioner of the County board of elections whose responsibility it is to examine the petitions and CERTIFY their accuracy and declare that a designee has fulfilled the requirement to be placed on the ballot. Since (s)he is often appointed to that position by being recommended by the political leader to the County legislature, (s)he must walk a very "thin" and precarious line during this period of time.

11. Most challengers lose in the primary. To challenge the party leadership with existing conditions is a "David and Goliath" experience.

Throughout this explanation you will note that the term DISENCHANTED is used to denote the party member who wishes to challenge a party designee. That label should not be attached to any party member who wishes to run for office.

Primaries were established to provide the voters at the election district level to participate in the SELECTION OF PARTY NOMINEES. Our citizens need more political education in this vital area.

Case History: Primary Election of 1978

In 1978, the Suffolk County Republican Party experienced a primary election that is worth discussing. That was a year of the election of a Governor, U.S. Senator, and U.S. Congressmen, as well as state assembly persons and senators.

Governor Hugh Carey was up for re-election. The Republican party decided to designate Parry B. Duryea of Suffolk County as the nominee for the governor's race. The political hierarchy of the party tried to get support of his candidacy from the conservative party.

The conservative party was willing to CROSS ENDORSE his candidacy if the Suffolk County Republican Party would cross endorse one of their party members for U.S. Congress in the First Congressional District. Otis G. Pike, who had been representing that district for the past 18 years, decided not to run again. The Suffolk County Republican Party acceded to that demand and set in motion a primary election.

At the Suffolk County Republican Party Convention, held in late May, the party leaders recommended to the committee persons in attendance that William Carney, a conservative party member and a member of the Suffolk County Legislature, be designated as the Republican nominee for U.S. Congress. The political leaders had done their homework and had obtained PROXY VOTES (committee persons GIVE their vote to the leader to do as HE PLEASES!).

Four Republican members who were interested in being considered as nominees were sidetracked by the party leaders and members. A DEAL HAD BEEN CUT!

An interesting note is that THREE of the Republicans had run as nominees in previous ELECTIONS against the incumbent Otis G. Pike (one of those was the author of this case history.)

Each of the four Republican members had to seek enough signatures of registered voters to earn a place on the primary election ballot in September. The deadline for submitting the designating petitions was in July. William Carney, the party nominee, enjoyed the support of many committee persons. He received 12,000 plus signatures to insure his place on the primary ballot. The author struggled to get 2200 signatures to get on the ballot. John Hart, James Catterson, and Jay Radway also got the required signatures.

During the long summer, the candidates met the public and several debates and discussed the issues. The press gave good coverage to "the Five Way Race for U.S. Congress." *Suffolk Life* and *Newsday* did extensive writing on the candidates, including what they stood for. The voters of Suffolk County had several viable candidates from whom to choose in the primary.

No voter in the congressional district could say (s)he had not been given adequate coverage of the race. Each candidate had articulated his positions in a meritorious manner. Now it was up to the voters of the First Congressional District to exercise their voting rights at the polling place in the primary election.

The voter turnout that primary day was dismal! Less than TWELVE PERCENT OF REPUBLICAN REGISTERED VOTERS showed up on that day. William Carney who had acquired over 12,000 signatures received a total vote of 4,800. Imagine the fact that 7,200 persons who had signed a designating petition did not even bother to go to the polling booth—despite visits by committee persons to their homes to have them sign the petition.

Carney was elected despite the fact that the other four candidates received over 65 per cent of the total votes cast! The four Republican candidates had to decide whether they would run on an Independent line. Had two of the candidates decided to make a decision to join forces, William Carney would have lost the election.

The important lesson to learn from this case history of a primary election is to try to EDUCATE voters when they are still in school to become aware of how important this election is and to help them understand why and how they can MAKE A DIFFERENCE in the political process. It was a very valuable lesson for the author. That is my motivation to write this political primer to help teachers to train our students.

The Designating Petition and Its Importance in the Political Process

Once the PARTY SLATE has been decided at the annual convention, designating petitions are prepared by the political leadership. These petitions contain several names of party nominees. These petitions have room for 20 signatures of registered voters. Each town committee person receives at least one designating petition to fill with the names of 20 registered voters in his/her election district.

Some towns like Brookhaven (largest in Suffolk County) have over 250 election districts. Two committee persons are in each election district. There are, therefore, over 500 town committee persons available to get 20 signatures each. If every committee person does his/her job, that adds up to 10,000 signatures. Most committee persons get the assigned petitions filled with signatures. Some get a few; others don't even both to go out to acquire any signatures.

In my experience as a committee person, I have acquired 60 or more signatures with the premise that a signature on a designating petition increases the chance that the signer will be likely to vote for that nominee in November.

Most committee persons keep going back to the same persons to get their petition filled with signatures. It takes about three hours to get the 20 signatures. The designating petitions are then bound together at party headquarters and numbered by page for easier reference. They have to be delivered to the County board of elections to be CERTIFIED by the commissioner of the board of election.

Designating petitions are the "NUTS and BOLTS" of the political party. It is because of them that a candidate gets on the ballot in a primary election and a November election. Designating petitions are kept on file at the County board of election. They are open to being perused by interested citizens as public information.

Visiting with the voters in the district can be a very rewarding experience for the committee person. It provides an opportunity to take the pulse of the district on how the voters feel about what is happening in the community; that can have a great effect in the coming election. A hard-working and effective committee person can be a big asset to the political party. Unfortunately, many do not take their role seriously, and as a result, political leaders get entrenched in their power base. Then candidates are sometimes chosen who are beholden to political leaders using the political process for self-serving purposes and favoritism.

Independent Nominating Petition - Sec. 6-140. ELECTION LAW

I, the undersigned, do hereby state that I am a registered voter of the political unit for which a nomination for public office is hereby being made, that my present place of residence is truly stated opposite my signature hereto, and that I do hereby nominate the following named person (or persons) as a candidate (or candidates) for nomination for public office (or public offices) to be voted for at the election to be held on the 8th day of November, 1994, and that I select the name TAX CUT NOW as the name of the independent body making the nomination (or nominations) and as the emblem of such body.

Name of Candidate(s)	Public Office	Place of Residence (also Post Office address if not identical)
George E. Pataki	Governor	Ienia, Route 9D Garrison, New York 10524
Elizabeth McCaughey	Lieutenant Governor	1111 Park Avenue, Apartment 13-C New York, New York 10128
Bernadette Castro	United States Senator	Quail Hill Road Lloyd Harbor, New York 11743
Dennis Vacco	Attorney General	61 Kenton Place Hamburg, New York 14075
Herbert I. London	Comptroller	2 Washington Square Village New York, New York 10012

I do hereby appoint William D. Powers, 1624 New York Post Road, Castleton, NY 12033; Joseph N. Mondello, 12 Shotgun Lane, Levittown, NY 11756; Margaret Soter, 15 Fenimore Road, Scarsdale, NY 10583; Clarence D. Rappleyea, P.O. Box 536-17, Chenango Lake Road, Norwich, NY 13815; Alexander Treadwell, P.O. Box 371, Westport, NY 12993; Thomas Reynolds, 28 Woodhaven Drive, Springville, NY 14141 and John F. Nolan, 8 Quevic Drive, Saratogo Springs, NY 12866 as a committee to fill vacancies in accordance with the provisions of the election law.

In witness whereof, I have hereunto set my hand, the day and year placed opposite my signature.

Date	Name of Signer Signature Required (printed name may be added)	Residence	Ward(if any) - or- Assembly District in NYC & Nassau	Elect. Dist.	Town or City - or - County in NYC
1.					
Printed Name					
2.					
Printed Name					
3.					
Printed Name					
4.					
Printed Name					
5.					
Printed Name					

Complete ONE of the Following

STATEMENT OF WITNESS

I, ______________________________ (name of witness) state: I am a duly qualified voter of the State of New York and I am also duly qualified to sign the petition. I now reside at ______________________________ (residence address, also post office address if not identical).

Each of the individuals whose names are subscribed to this petition sheet containing __________ (fill in number) signatures, subscribed the same in my presence on the dates above indicated and identified himself to be the individual who signed this sheet.

I understand that this statement will be accepted for all purposes as the equivalent of an affidavit and, if it contains a material false statement, shall subject me to the same penalties as if I had been duly sworn.

Dated:____________________ ______________________________ (Signature)

WITNESS IDENTIFICATION INFORMATION: The following information must be completed prior to filing with the board of elections in order for this petition sheet to be valid.

Election District	Ward(if any) - or- Assembly District in NYC & Nassau	Town or City	County

NOTARY PUBLIC OR COMMISSIONER OF DEEDS

On the dates above indicated before me personally came each of the voters whose signatures appear on this petition sheet containing_______ (fill in number) signatures, who signed same in my presence and who, being by me duly sworn, each for himself, said that the foregoing statement made and subscribed by him, was true.

Dated:____________________ ______________________________ (Signature and Official Title of Officer Administering Oath)

Fort
Orange
Press

QUESTIONS TO ASK DURING INTERVIEW OF TOWN COMMITTEE PERSON

1. How do you become a committee person?

2. Why did you decide to become a committee person?

3. How old do you have to be to become a committee person? Are you elected? For how long?

4. Do you earn a salary as a committee person? When do you run for election?

5. What is a designating petition? How do you decide as to who to get to sign it?

6. How does a candidate get on the ballot?

7. What is primary election? When is it held?

8. Why do so few voters participate in primary elections?

9. What are your responsibilities as a committee person?

10. Do you like your job? Why?

11. What is a town leader? How does he become a leader?

12. What would you suggest for us to do to become involved in politics?

13. What kinds of experiences have you had as a committee person?

14. Have you met any interesting persons in your role of committee person?

15. What do you try to do as a committee person to get voters to go to the polls on election day?

16. What is an election district?

17. What is the responsibility of the County board of elections?

18. How does a board of election commissioner get his/her position?

19. Have you ever thought of running for office?

20. What do you look for in a candidate that wants to run for a political office?

Town Government Organization

Students are now ready to be introduced to the town government and how it is organized. Townships throughout New York State vary in geographic size and population, but organization is similar in nature.

The Supervisor

The chief executive of the town is the SUPERVISOR. (S)he is elected for a term of two years (Note: some townships are now electing a supervisor for a term of four years). (S)he also presides at town board meetings. His position is FULL-TIME. (S)he has the authority to make appointments to various departments in the town. (S)he tries to select persons that are well qualified for the job. Occasionally, (s)he might appoint someone recommended by the town leader that helped him/her get elected. This is a "PAYOFF" to a person who did a favor for the town leader.

The Town Clerk

(S)he attends town board meetings to record the PROCEEDINGS of the meeting, keeps records of CONTRACTS AND AGREEMENTS the town makes and issues LICENSES, PERMITS AND CERTIFICATES OF BIRTH, MARRIAGE, AND DEATH. (S)he is ELECTED FOR A FOUR-YEAR TERM.

The Deputy Supervisor

(S)he represents the supervisor when (s)he is unavailable and assists the supervisor in the administration of the town government. Duties of the deputy supervisor include:

1. Handling media relations (radio, newspaper, TV).
2. Issuing periodic PRESS RELEASES to notify town residents of changes in town ORDINANCES and POLICIES.
3. Preparing brochures, displays and announcements of town-sponsored events.
4. Interviewing prospective candidates for positions in town government and recommends candidate to town board.
5. Conducts labor relations such as CONTRACT NEGOTIATIONS between the town government and unions representing town employees. APPOINTED by the town supervisor.

The Town Board

The town board is the legislative branch of the town government. The PRESIDING OFFICER of the town board is the SUPERVISOR. His/her office prepares the AGENDA of the meetings that are held REGULARLY on a monthly basis.

The town board also holds SPECIAL MEETINGS throughout the year, whenever situations arise that require these meetings to be held. ALL MEETINGS are announced ahead of time, so that the PUBLIC can be notified. ALL TOWN BOARD MEETINGS MUST BE HELD BEFORE THE GENERAL PUBLIC.

RESIDENTS of the town, wishing to know when and where meetings are held, have to read their local newspapers, where these meetings are printed in the PUBLIC NOTICES section. They can also call the town supervisor's office to ask where, when, and what time the scheduled meeting will be held.

The AGENDA is prepared, in advance, by the town supervisor so that the public can know what TOWN MATTERS will be discussed at that meeting. Citizens, who wish to speak at these town meetings, are asked to fill a CARD to indicate that they wish to address the town board about what is being addressed by the board. At a town board meeting are town employees who assist the town board to record the PROCEEDINGS of the meeting.

The TOWN LAWYER is usually at town board meetings. (S)he is there to give the town board legal advice when necessary. The town board must know what town ORDINANCES are in existence and if NEW ORDINANCES have any effect on existing ORDINANCES. The town lawyer is APPOINTED by the TOWN SUPERVISOR and is available to him and town board members when LEGAL QUESTIONS arise either at town board meetings or other times. (S)he has other LEGAL assistants to help him keep the town officials informed about legal matters. At times, the town is SUED by citizens who feel they have been WRONGED by the town government. The town lawyer prepares a CASE to defend the town government against the citizen who is SUING the town government.

In CASES where the town government is being SUED, the citizen is the PLAINTIFF and the town government is the DEFENDANT. At other times, the town government can charge a citizen with breaking TOWN ORDINANCES. The town lawyer then prepares a CASE against the citizen who is accused of breaking a town ordinance. In this situation, the town lawyer becomes the PROSECUTOR and the citizen becomes the DEFENDANT. The citizen, in both CASES, needs to hire a LAWYER (ATTORNEY) to "PRESS HIS/HER CASE."

The town board members are called COUNCIL PERSONS. They are ELECTED for a TERM OF FOUR YEARS. There are usually SIX MEMBERS on the board. They are ELECTED ON ODD YEARS (1995, 1997, 1999, etc.). The board is divided into two GROUPS OF THREE. This means that three board members are ELECTED during one ODD YEAR ELECTION, 1995, and the other three board members are elected during another ODD YEAR ELECTION, 1997.

In this manner, voters vote for three board members at a time and this results in having three board members remain on the board to run during the NEXT ELECTION. This PREVENTS a situation from occurring where it could happen that if ALL SIX COUNCIL PERSONS RAN AT THE SAME TIME, THEY COULD ALL BE DEFEATED AND WE WOULD HAVE SIX NEW COUNCILMEN, ALL STARTING OFF WITH NO EXPERIENCE IN TOWN GOVERNMENT, AND NO ONE THERE TO HELP THEM GET OFF TO A GOOD START. By STAGGERING the ELECTION of town councilmen, it assures the citizens of the town that there will be at least THREE members who can assist the three NEW MEMBERS OF THE TOWN BOARD.

Each COUNCIL PERSON has one vote. Council persons introduce and vote on legislation. They address the needs of the residents who are sometimes called CONSTITUENTS. They are also assigned to various COMMITTEES. These committees hold public hearings to give the public opportunities to give input into ORDINANCES (laws) that are being considered by the town government. These new ordinances could relate to building a new road, purchasing land for a town recreation area, dealing with the environment, etc.

Town council persons also make on-site visits of areas needing their personal observation. Town beaches are inspected for EROSION. Town parks are visited to see how they are being maintained, town departments are visited to see how they are functioning on behalf of the citizens. They are invited to speak at clubs, civic associations and other community organizations to keep citizens informed on what is happening in town government. town councilmen must be well informed on how the money ALLOCATED for the town budget is being spent. Council persons hold STRATEGY SESSIONS to discuss future needs of the town. They devote many hours to their responsibilities and they need to be visible to the town residents.

NOTE TO TEACHER: A visit to a scheduled town board meeting will be very beneficial to the students. Have students prepare questions to ask members of the town board when they make the visit.

The Town Budget

The town board is responsible for reviewing and approving the annual town budget which is prepared by the town supervisor and the various departments in town government. The APPROPRIATIONS (expenditures, money that will be spent in the following year) needed, determine how much TAXES will have to be paid by the town residents. There are BUDGET HEARINGS held at the time of the BUDGET REVIEW. There is usually much interest shown by town residents at town budget time.

Town Departments and Services

There are a number of departments in the town government. These departments help to provide SERVICES that residents need to carry on their daily lives.

Public Information

The public information office prepares and sends out information on all areas of town government. They prepare BROCHURES, NEWSLETTERS, PRESS RELEASES AND PUBLIC SERVICE ANNOUNCEMENTS. They also answer phone calls from town residents seeking Information on what department they need to resolve a problem.

Division of Youth Bureau

This department is assigned the responsibility for planning and coordinating activities and services for youths and their families. Programs of the youth bureau include:

1. Providing a sanctuary program for runaway and homeless youths.

2. Providing counseling services to youths and their families as needed.

3. Providing preventive education programs on drug and alcohol abuse.

4. Assisting students experiencing school attendance problems (PINS).

5. Provides vocational services to help youths choose worthwhile careers.

6. Maintaining a COALITION of corporate volunteers to help youths find job (referred to as INTERFACE).

7. Providing funding for community based YOUTH SERVICE AGENCIES. These agencies provide recreation, counseling and youth development services.

The youth board is comprised of adults and youth who volunteer to serve a two-year term. They are appointed by the town board.

Assessor's Office

This town official determines a money value for each piece of property in the town. This figure (assessment) is used to determine the amount of taxes to be paid by the PROPERTY OWNER. The value of your property is determined by:

1. The size of your land area

2. The amount of living space in your home

3. The location of your home

4. Other fixed buildings (garage, tool shed, etc.)

5. A swimming pool

If a resident feels the ASSESSOR has assessed the property too high, (s)he may file a GRIEVANCE and have his property REASSESSED. GRIEVANCE DAY is held ONE DAY A YEAR IN MAY.

Finance Department

This department is responsible for maintaining accurate records of the town's MONETARY TRANSACTIONS, including payroll. The department head is a COMMISSIONER, who helps prepare the town budget and works with an outside PUBLIC ACCOUNTING FIRM to AUDIT financial records each year.

Division of Data Processing

This division is responsible for the storage of the data and information compiled by the town. It makes the data available to other departments in the town government.

Purchasing Division

This department purchases all supplies necessary for the operation of the town government, including paper supplies, vehicles (trucks, autos, heavy equipment) furniture, etc. It also handles CONTRACTS for town VENDORS, construction companies and FRANCHISES.

Receiver of Taxes

This official is responsible for collecting the taxes for the following government agencies:

1. County

2. Town

3. School districts in the town

4. Special districts

(S)he is also responsible for DISTRIBUTING the taxes appropriately. (S)he is ELECTED by the voters for a FOUR YEAR TERM. Each year s(he) prepares the tax bill to mail out to all PROPERTY OWNERS throughout the town. (S)he works with the town assessor's office to see if there are any changes in the assessment of any property, which would change the taxes charged to that property. Tax bills are usually sent in early December. Taxpayers can pay their bill by mail or go to the tax receiver's office. Taxpayers can divide their bill in half, paying half in December and the other half in May, with no penalty or extra charge.

STATEMENT OF TAXES

DECEMBER 1, 1996 thru NOVEMBER 30, 1997 TAX LEVY
TOWN OF BROOKHAVEN, SUFFOLK COUNTY, NEW YORK
TAXABLE STATUS DATE MARCH 1, 1996
TAXES BECOME A LIEN DECEMBER 1, 1996

ESTIMATED STATE AID
COUNTY
TOWN
SCHOOL
SEWER

MAKE FUNDS PAYABLE TO:

F. DANIEL MOLONEY
RECEIVER OF TAXES
250 EAST MAIN STREET
PORT JEFFERSON, NEW YORK 11777

OFFICE PAYMENT HOUSE
MON.TO FRI. 9 A.M. TO 4 P.M.
PHONE 516-473-0236

IMPORTANT
FOR SCHOOL INQUIRIES CALL

IF PROPERTY HAS BEEN SOLD TRANSFERRED AFTER MARCH 1996, PLEASE FORWARD THE STATEMENT TO THE NEW OWNER OR RETURN TO THIS OFFICE

SUFFOLK COUNTY TAX MAP NUMBER UNIT STREET BLOCK LOT	DESCRIPTION OF PROPERTY	EXEMPTION DESCRIPTION	EXEMPT CODE	EXEMPTION
TYPE ACREAGE TAX CODE ROLL SECTION				

PHYSICAL ADDRESS	BANK AND MORTGAGE NUMBERS	BILL NUMBER	LAND ASSESSMENT	TOTAL ASSESSMENT

OWNER AS OF TAXABLE STATUS DATE MARCH 1, 1996

TAX BILLING ADDRESS

John and Jane Doe
123 Heaven Avenue
Ronkonkoma, New York 11779

WHEN PAYING IN PERSON BRING ENTIRE BILL

LEVY DESCRIPTION	EXEMPT CODES	TAXABLE VALUE ADJUSTED BY EXEMPTIONS	TAX RATE PER $100	TAX AMOUNT
SCHOOL DISTRICT SACHEM		2,500	98.555	
LIBRARY DISTRICT SACHEM		2,500		4.20
COUNTY OF SUFFOLK		2,500	27.621	
TOWN GENERAL		2,500	4.239	
HIGHWAY TOWN WIDE		2,500	1.953	
HIGHWAY OUTSIDE INCORPORATED VILLAGES		2,500	.564	
BROOKHAVEN REUSE CYCLING FAMILY				225.00
FIRE DISTRICT RONKONKOMA		2,500	7.032	
LIGHTING DISTRICT		2,500	.920	
REAL PROPERTY TAX LAW ARTICLE 7		2,500	1.832	

DUPLICATE

FIRST HALF TAX	SECOND HALF TAX	TOTAL TAX
DECEMBER 1, 1996, PAYABLE WITHOUT PENALTY TO JANUARY 10, 1997. REVERSE SIDE FOR PENALTY SCHEDULE	DUE DECEMBER 1,1996, PAYABLE WITHOUT PENALTY TO MAY 31, 1997, SEE REVERSE SIDE FOR PENALTY SCHEDULE AND COUNTY TREASURERS NOTICE	THIS TOTAL TAX MAY BE PAID IN ONE OR TWO INSTALLMENTS

SECOND PAYMENT ( )
DUE DECEMBER 1, 1996
PAYABLE WITHOUT PENALTY
TO MAY 31, 1997 MAY BE
PAID WITH FIRST PAYMENT

WHEN PAYING BY MAIL DETACH FOR 2nd HALF PAYMENT (RETURN BOTH STUBS FOR TOTAL PAYMENT)

TOTAL TAX

TOWN OF BROOKHAVEN
1996-1997 TAX LEVY

ITEM NUMBER

MAKE FUNDS PAYABLE TO: F. DANIEL MOLONEY, RECEIVER OF TAXES

SECOND PAYMENT

OWNER AS OF TAXABLE STATUS DATE MARCH 1, 1996

TAX BILLING ADDRESS

2

______

PENALTY ______

______

WRITE ITEM NUMBER ON CHECK
MAIL WITH PAYMENT

PAYOR ______

( ) CHECK HERE IF YOU WISH A RECEIPT

FIRST PAYMENT ( )
DUE DECEMBER 1, 1996
PAYABLE WITHOUT PENALTY
TO JANUARY 10, 1997

WHEN PAYING BY MAIL DETACH FOR 1ST HALF PAYMENT (RETURN BOTH STUBS FOR TOTAL PAYMENT)

TOTAL TAX

TOWN OF BROOKHAVEN
1996-1997 TAX LEVY

ITEM NUMBER

MAKE FUNDS PAYABLE TO: F. DANIEL MOLONEY, RECEIVER OF TAXES

FIRST PAYMENT

OWNER AS OF TAXABLE STATUS DATE MARCH 1, 1996

TAX BILLING ADDRESS

1

______

PENALTY ______

______

WRITE ITEM NUMBER ON CHECK
MAIL WITH PAYMENT

PAYOR ______

( ) CHECK HERE IF YOU WISH A RECEIPT

Superintendent of Highways

This official is charged with the responsibility of maintaining all town roads, building sidewalks, and managing road repair, leaf collection, and snow removal. In addition, s(he) maintains GREENHOUSES and a LEAF COMPOSTING PROGRAM and conducts an ECOLOGY EDUCATION PROGRAM, which explores ways to reclaim OLD LANDFILL sites as PARK FACILITIES. S(he) is ELECTED FOR A TWO-YEAR TERM.

Personnel Division

The personnel division administers all aspects of personnel activity including, but not limited to, employment, labor relations and employee benefits. The division is responsible for maintaining records regarding these important functions:

1. Keeping records of vacation days taken by employees.
2. Keeping records of employee earnings and taxes paid to federal and state government.
3. Recording days employees are not present at work.
4. Assisting employees regarding health benefits.
5. Maintaining records of funds deposited in pension fund of employees.

Department of Housing, Community Development, and Intergovernmental Affairs

A COMMISSIONER, appointed by the town board, heads this department, which is concerned with the following responsibilities:

1. Improving sub-standard living conditions.

2. Revitalizing commercial centers.

3. Providing programs to train the unemployed and help them find jobs.

4. Managing and coordinating federal and state housing programs.

Department of Parks, Recreation and Human Services

A town board-appointed commissioner heads the department, which has THREE separate divisions:

Human Resources Division

This division carries out the following responsibilities:

1. Supervising and coordinating senior citizen clubs located throughout the town.

2. Promoting worthwhile programs and activities for the senior citizens who visit the various clubs.

3. Preparing a newsletter that is mailed to senior citizens to inform them of activities that are coming up in the future.

4. Providing HOME AIDS to assist senior citizens who need help at home.

Maintenance Services Division

This division is responsible for:

1. Caring for all town-owned property.

2. Supplying a FULL-TIME STAFF of plumbers, painters, carpenters, electricians, and ground maintenance crew to keep the town-owned property operating efficiently.

3. Maintaining town buildings, marinas, parks, and town-owned swimming pools.

Leisure Services Division

This division:

1. Develops leisure programs for all town residents—youths, senior citizens and the handicapped (like bowling, basketball, and softball leagues) and sponsors SUMMER RECREATION PROGRAMS at town parks, pools, beaches, and

schools. These PROGRAMS are well-supervised. There is also a council for the arts, which plans and coordinates MUSIC, DANCE, and FINE ARTS PROGRAMS.

2. The TOWN HISTORIAN keeps historical records and provides students with lectures on town history.

Department of Planning and Development

This department has FOUR DIVISIONS, which are concerned with improving our environment and to attract business and industry to the town. A town board-appointed commissioner is responsible for supervising all FOUR DIVISIONS.

Building Division

This division has an important role to play in the town community. Well-trained persons are needed in this important division, which accomplishes the following:

1. Issues building permits for NEW BUILDINGS and ADDITIONS TO OLD BUILDINGS.

2. Inspects buildings as they are being built to make certain that BUILDING CODES, established by the town board, are followed. Foundations of buildings, electrical wiring, plumbing, and cesspools are carefully inspected for health and safety reasons.

3. Issues a CERTIFICATE OF OCCUPANCY when the building has been inspected and found to be safe for the owner to inhabit.

Economic Development Division

This division:

1. Provides services to help existing businesses to succeed.

2. Tries to encourage new businesses to establish themselves in the town.

An influx of businesses increases job opportunities and increases the economic wealth of the town; it also increases the taxable income of the town.

Environmental Protection Division

This division:

1. Monitors sensitive areas of the environment (underground water sources).

2. Monitors shorelines where shellfishing grounds are located (pollution hazards).
3. Seeks ways to educate citizens on the importance of protecting the ecology.

Planning Division

This division:

1. Reviews all existing town maps and sites for the future

improvement of any UNINCORPORATED areas within the town.

2. Reviews and amends town zoning laws.

3. Zoning laws divide town properties into:

   a. RESIDENTIAL ZONES. Only homes can be built in these zones. Property on which a building is going to be built needs to have a certain amount of square feet—one-quarter acre, one-half acre, one acre, etc. Town zoning laws will specify how large a piece of property has to be in order to build a home upon it.

   b. BUSINESS ZONES. These are land areas in which businesses can be established.

   c. INDUSTRIAL ZONES. These are land areas in which FACTORIES OR MANUFACTURING COMPANIES can build their buildings.

These zoning laws are established to provide a well-planned community, where citizens can live in safe areas and enjoy pleasant surroundings, away from noisy, heavy traffic areas of industrial development.

Public Safety Department

Public safety has FIVE DIVISIONS that help insure the safety of town residents. A commissioner heads the department and is appointed by the town board.

Animal Shelter Division

This division insures the safety of town residents by the following means:

1. Investigating complaints of dangerous animals.

2. Capturing dangerous animals.

3. Trying to find adoptive homes for captured animals that have been abandoned by owners.

4. Conducting a SPAY/NEUTER clinic for residents' pets.

Division of Traffic Safety / Streetlight Maintenance

1. Conducts traffic surveys to determine where traffic signs and signals need to be installed.

2. Conducts speaking engagements to educate residents of the town on road safety and the dangers of driving DWI (driving while intoxicated).

3. Installs streetlights to insure greater safety in neighborhoods.

4. Maintains the streetlights and traffic signals.

Fire Prevention Division

This division insures public safety in the following ways:

1. It periodically inspects buildings to insure their safety.

2. It investigates fires to determine if ARSON took place.

3. It conducts ongoing education program for town residents on fire prevention.

Code Enforcement Division

Administered by a town-appointed commissioner, this division:

1. Investigates complaints filed by town residents about someone breaking a town law.

2. Supervises town safety officers which include Bay constables, park police, and auxiliary police.

Motor Vehicle Control Division

This division:

1. Purchases town vehicles (autos, trucks).

2. Repairs town vehicles.

3. Maintains fuel supplies for town vehicles.

Waste Management Department

The waste management department was established to undertake a solid waste management program that coordinates PLANNING, DEVELOPMENT, and ENFORCEMENT of sound waste management policies and practices that satisfy the requirements of existing laws. The waste management department is responsible for the following tasks:

1. It deals with litter created by non-caring residents or visitors to the town.

2. It maintains landfill operations and RECYCLING.

3. It is empowered to license WASTE HAULERS.

4. It supervises the landfill and related facilities.

5. It establishes fees for use of landfill facility.

6. It prohibits or restricts hazardous waste brought to landfill facility.

7. It educates residents on how to reduce WASTE.

8. Lastly, it plans efficient ways to collect waste materials.

Zoning Board of Appeals

The zoning board of appeals has SEVEN town board-appointed members, one of whom is the CHAIRPERSON. They meet to discuss requests made by town residents to make a change in the status of their property that is different from what the town zoning laws allow.

For example, some might want to extend their building close to the property line that divides their property from their neighbor. Others might want to build a store in a residential zone. These requests are formally presented to the zoning board of appeals. They DELIBERATE and decide whether to approve the request of the town resident.

If they approve the request, the town resident is given a VARIANCE (exception to the existing town zoning laws). People who are effected by town resident request are notified and invited to attend the public hearing held by the zoning board of appeals. This is a very sensitive area of government. The decision made by the board often leaves someone unhappy with their decision.

ZONING BOARD OF APPEALS MEMBERS SERVE FOR A TERM OF FIVE YEARS! They receive an ANNUAL SALARY FOR THEIR SERVICES TO THE TOWN. Board members usually receive this appointment at the recommendation of the TOWN LEADER as a reward for their work on behalf of the political party.

TEACHER'S NOTE: A member of this board would be a very interesting speaker to invite to the politically astute class. Questions should be prepared by teacher and class to ask the invited board member.

Department of Law

The chief executive officer of this department is the TOWN ATTORNEY. (S)he is APPOINTED by the TOWN

BOARD. (S)he is appointed on the basis of administrative experience and must be a practicing attorney. The town attorney usually has two deputy attorneys to assist him/her in carrying out his/her responsibilities. Duties of the town attorney include:

1. Giving legal advice to all town departments, agencies, and offices as well as special boards established by the town board (example: zoning board of appeals).

2. Preparing or approving all leases and land acquisitions on behalf of the town.

3. Preparing, approving, and/or processing all contracts entered into by the town.

4. Attending all necessary conferences involving departments, rendering legal advice during the term of such contracts.

5. Preparing, reviewing, and recommending all local town laws, amendments, and related public notices.

6. Preparing and processing all special agreements entered into by the town government.

7. Conducting legal research and giving legal opinions.

8. Reviewing petitions and exhibits for changes of zone and special use permits.

9. Reviewing all applications and petitions relating to special district improvements or extensions.

DEPARTMENT: LAW

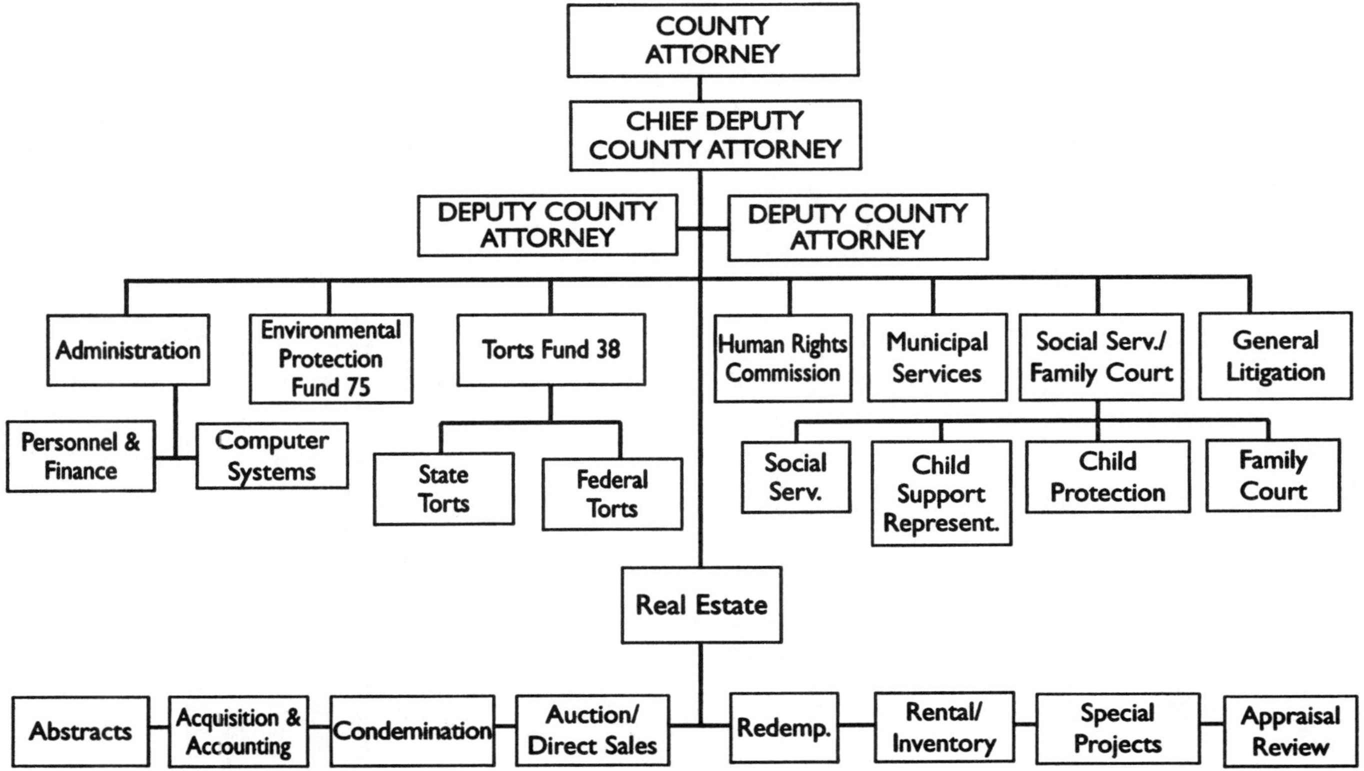

10. Representing the town in all legal matters in court.

11. Prosecuting violators or town laws (ordinances).

12. Starting, defending, or appealing actions in the name of the town.

13. Hiring private consultants, experts and other parties when needed, with approval of town board.

Understanding the Tax Bill

Each year town residents receive a tax bill sent to them by the town tax receiver. This tax bill contains TAXES to be paid to several GOVERNMENTAL AGENCIES. A copy of a typical town tax bill should be reproduced and reviewed by the teacher. A FACSIMILE (COPY) can be acquired from the tax receiver's office.

Students should be made aware of the number of governmental agencies that receive taxes to conduct their services to the citizens. The tax receiver, upon receiving the taxes paid by the town residents, distribute them to agencies listed on the bill. These include: 1) fire district 2) school district 3) lighting district 4) library district 5) town highway department 6) town government and 7) County government. The tax receiver's office acts as a COLLECTION AGENCY for other governing districts.

Many citizens, unfortunately, do not carefully examine their tax bill and often refer to the amount of taxes they pay to various government districts incorrectly. Students,

Town of Islip Organizational Chart

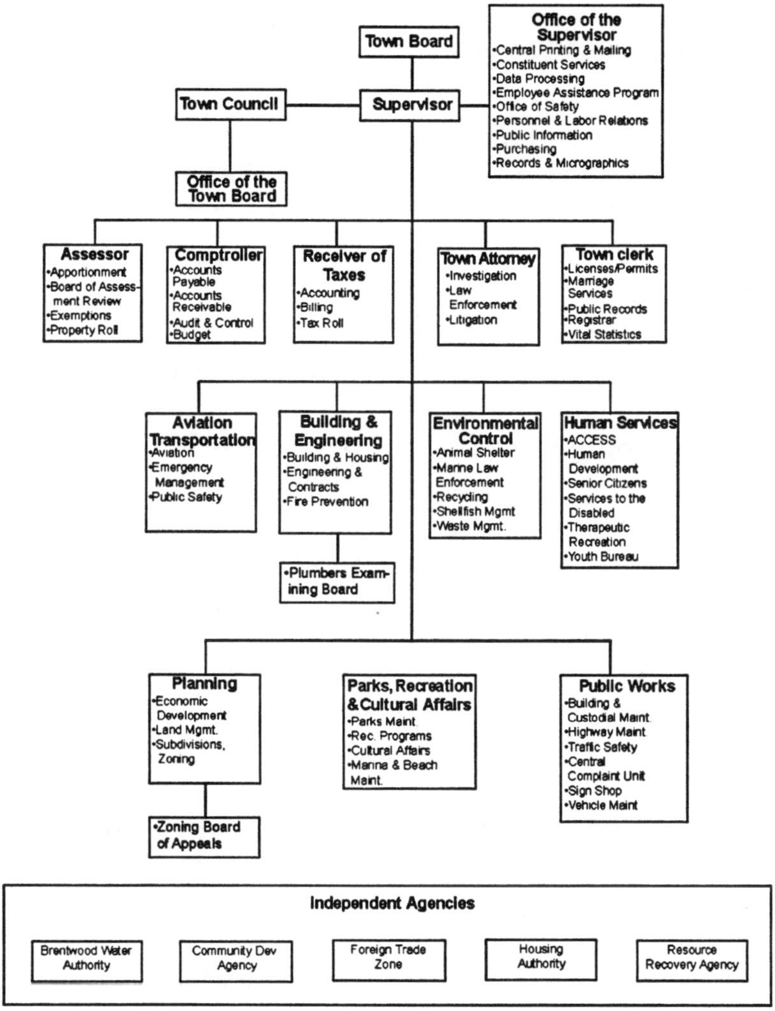

after reviewing the tax bill, can discuss how much money is spent on their education (school TAXES) at the local level and develop an appreciation of how much money is invested in their education.

Judicial Branch of Town Government

The number of district court judges in a town is determined by the size and population of the town. District court judges are ELECTED by town residents. Their term of office is SIX YEARS. Their responsibilities to the people are:

1. Helping interpret town laws to citizens of town.

2. Trying and punishing lawbreakers with trial by jury.

   a. A citizen can be accused of committing a FELONY (serious crimes like armed robbery, murder, EMBEZZLING (stealing) money from a bank or government agency).

   b. A citizen can be accused of a less serious crime (property damage, petty robbery, serious traffic violations, DWI). These are called MISDEMEANORS.

3. Presenting accused citizen with what (s)he is being charged with, asking DEFENDANT to plead "GUILTY" or "NOT GUILTY." This is an INDICTMENT (charges).

   a. If the accused pleads "not guilty" a TRIAL DATE is set up and accused is asked to get an ATTORNEY to defend him/her.

   b. If an accused citizen cannot afford an attorney, the COURT assigns a lawyer approved by the accused.

4. A JURY is EMPANELLED (selected) for the purpose of hearing the EVIDENCE and determining whether the accused is "guilty" or "not guilty."

TEACHER'S NOTE: A practicing trial attorney could be invited to the class to speak to the students about courtroom procedures during criminal trials. A visit to a district court is highly recommended.

SUMMARY OF TOWN GOVERNMENT

Teacher should prioritize what should be remembered by students at end of the study unit. Many new terms and concepts have been introduced during this study unit. Should a unit test be given? If so, teacher should use discretion. Consider letting students use their notes in taking the test. It can be used to REINFORCE what has been taught in class. GLOSSARY TERMS THAT NEED TO BE REVIEWED:

1. Name Recognition
2. Nominee
3. Qualify
4. Campaign
5. Designating Petition
6. Primary Election
7. Circulate
8. Screening a candidate
9. Autocratic
10. Variance
11. Arson
12. Political Process
13. Agenda
14. Patronage
15. Bossism
16. Centralized
17. Budget
18. Ordinance
19. Strategy Sessions
20. Appropriations
21. Embezzle
22. Coalition
23. Grievance
24. Assessor
25. Economic
26. Felony
27. Misdemeanor
28. Indict
29. Impanel
30. Plaintiff
31. Defendant

Teachers ought to motivate students to write essays on the following topics, being prepared to read them to the rest of the class:

1. Why it is important to be a politically astute citizen.

2. What I learned from my field trip to the town board.

3. What I learned from the town committee person visit to visit our class.

4. What I remember about our study of village government.

5. Why it is important to study our tax bill.

6. How I feel about studying our town and village government organization.

Chapter 3
County Government Organization

County government is more extensive than the town government just explored by the students. Students need to know that County government serves the needs of a number of towns that cannot provide the services which the County government provides.

As in town government, the County government is likewise divided into three branches: executive, legislative, and judicial. The geographic area of a County is larger in area than a town. The population is typically greater in number. The problems, while similar in nature, are more complex.

The political picture begins to change on the County level. In village and town government, the elected officials are easier to contact and the citizens talk, more often than not, directly to the elected officials. On the County level, a citizen begins to find that the elected officials are more difficult to contact directly. Legislative aides are staff members who do the initial interactions with citizens and try to resolve constituent problems without the intervention of elected officials.

As the students begin to be exposed to County government, it is important for the teacher to explain that although elected officials are difficult to reach, they are not inaccessible. In a democracy, the further away the seat of government, the more it is necessary to exercise persistence and patience. In the time ahead, the teacher should plan to have several County government officials visit the class, also noting the various field trips that students should make.

It is strongly recommended that 40 weeks of one period per week should be allotted to the study of County government. It is important for the teacher to plan on establishing priorities as to what should students should be exposed. The teacher should not attempt to cover too much. There is the danger of not seeing "the forest because the trees are in the way." Too much content and/or detail would tend to distract the students and diminish their natural curiosity.

There are many services provided by County government. The major departments in County government should be outlined and discussed. Personnel from these departments would be effective guest speakers for the students to interview. Field trips to a County court trial, a County legislature meeting, and one or two County departments (health department, district attorney, social services, and/or citizens' affairs) should be considered seriously to enhance the teacher's weekly class lessons. Students are greatly influenced by these guest speakers and field trips to County government offices. Teacher should prepare a list of relevant questions for the students to ask the guest speakers. Later, with the teacher's list acting as a model, the students will learn how to formulate their own questions, making a visit from a guest speaker and a field trip to a County government office more meaningful.

County Government Elected Officials

In County government, there are a number of ELECTED Officials, but many more are APPOINTED to their positions. Many APPOINTED officials acquire their positions through the taking of COMPETITIVE TESTS administered and scheduled by the CIVIL SERVICE COMMISSION. These tests are scheduled periodically and a civil service list is established. A good test score doesn't assure that the person who got the high score will be given a position. For example if there is one position open and three people score 100, 99, and 98, the person getting the 100 gets the job and the other two do not. But if the person who made the 100 doesn't take the position, the one with the 99 gets it.

There are many good opportunities for challenging and rewarding positions in government. Throughout the United States, millions of citizens work for some level of government or another. There is some degree of JOB SECURITY and good to excellent opportunities for advancement. Educational background helps the position-seeker to do well on the civil service tests and to also do well on JOB INTERVIEWS which accompany the taking of the test.

The remaining appointed positions are filled by those elected. Usually these people have helped the elected person during the campaign. Students should realize that elected leaders need trustworthy persons around them when they carry out their responsibilities to the electorate.

A person who has helped the elected official is generally politically astute and has good background in interpersonal relations (dealing with constituent problems) and also has a good education in political science. People running for office need strong personalities around them that will tell him/her how things REALLY ARE so that (s)he can correct the error of his/her ways with a minimum of loss of public approval.

Students interested in becoming politically astute need to expose themselves to professional courses in psychology, sociology, and administration. They also need to become street-wise, something not learned in formal education, but in working in the public domain and by doing a lot of listening!

There are usually SIX elected officials in County Government. They are:

1. The County comptroller

2. The County treasurer

3. The County clerk

4. The County sheriff

5. The district attorney

6. The County executive

Each of these elected officials are elected for a four-year term, but do not run at the same time. For example, the County executive, County sheriff, and County comptroller will run in 1995, 1999, and so on; whereas the County treasurer, County clerk, and district attorney will run in 1997, 2001, 2005, etc. In this manner, the electorate is afforded the opportunity to ELECT three of the office-holders every two years instead of all six in one election. The voter can concentrate better on THREE candidates instead of SIX!

Each of these six candidates carries out very important responsibilities. Let us now outline each department that the elected candidates administer during their term of office.

The County Comptroller

Although this elected official receives little or no exposure in the MEDIA (newspapers, radio, television, and magazines), (s)he has a very responsible role. The County comptroller is authorized to:

1. Examine, AUDIT, and verify all books, records, accounts kept by the various administrative units, County departments, offices of officials paid from County funds.

2. Verify, approve, and process the County payroll.

3. Examine and approve for payment all contracts, purchase orders, and other documents.

4. Prepare financial statements showing how money was spent by the County government.

5. Try to acquire loans at the lowest rate of interest when the County needs to borrow money.

6. Examine the financial records of County departments to see that money is being spent properly.

COUNTY COMPTROLLER DEPARTMENT

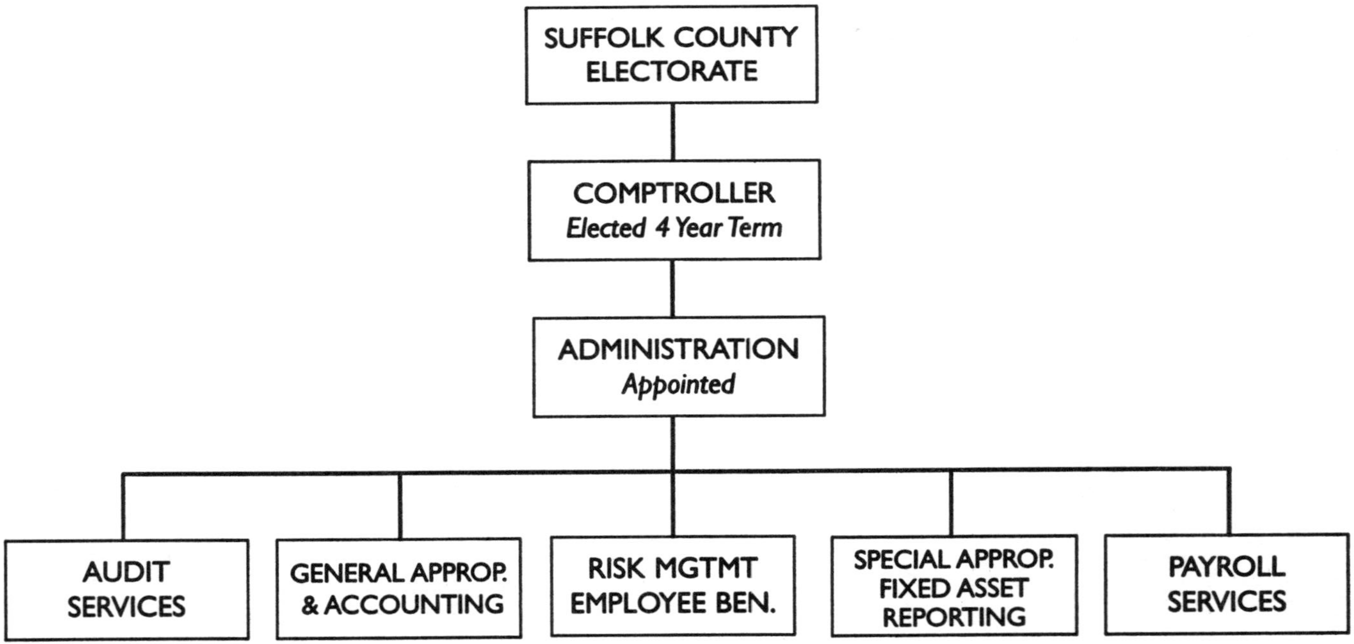

NOTE: A number of staff members are APPOINTED. Most are chosen by Competitive Civil Service Exams.

It is easy to see why this fiscal officer is elected and directly answerable to the citizens of the County. (S)he must be well trained in accounting and business management and be a person of HIGH INTEGRITY!

The County Treasurer

This elected official heads the department known as FINANCE and TAXATION. This department receives most of the money belonging or handled by the County. The responsibilities of the treasurer are:

1. Collecting all taxes, fees and other revenue payable to the County.

2. Depositing all funds collected from taxes in well-established banks and tries to earn money from INTEREST at the best rate being offered by banks.

3. Auditing all town tax receiver accounts.

4. Maintaining all town tax assessment and tax ARREARS records.

5. Disposing of (selling) all tax DELINQUENT properties.

6. Maintaining and updating the entire County TAX MAP.

7. Providing public agencies and individuals with information, forms, and reports on all aspects of real property.

8. Training County assessors how to assess (evaluate) property.

DEPARTMENT: FINANCE & TAXATION

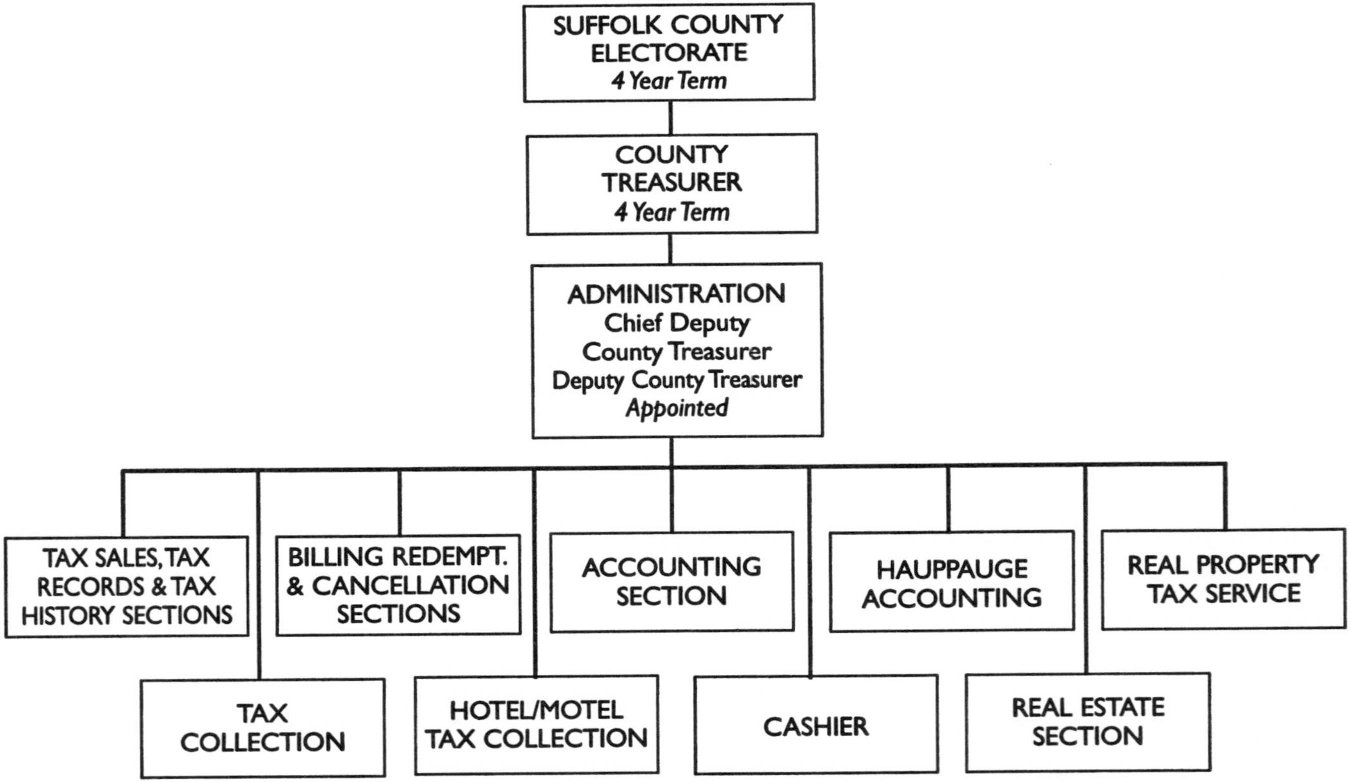

The County Clerk

The primary role of the County clerk is to maintain PUBLIC RECORDS including: deeds, mortgages, court judgments, certificates of incorporation, and other official documents. The County clerk is responsible for:

1. Recording and filing documents related to County business.

2. Recording deeds to property, making them available to interested people.

3. Collecting mortgage taxes for the County.

4. Issuing passport and naturalization papers.

5. Storing, in secure and safe locations, important land maps, historical charters, and other historical papers (ARCHIVES).

6. Making frequent public appearances to inform the citizens of the role of the County clerk's office.

NOTE. The County clerk would be a worthwhile guest speaker for the class.

The County Sheriff

The County sheriff has many important responsibilities during a four-year term of office. Many people have asked why a sheriff's department exists in the County in the first

SUFFOLK COUNTY CLERK
Organization Chart

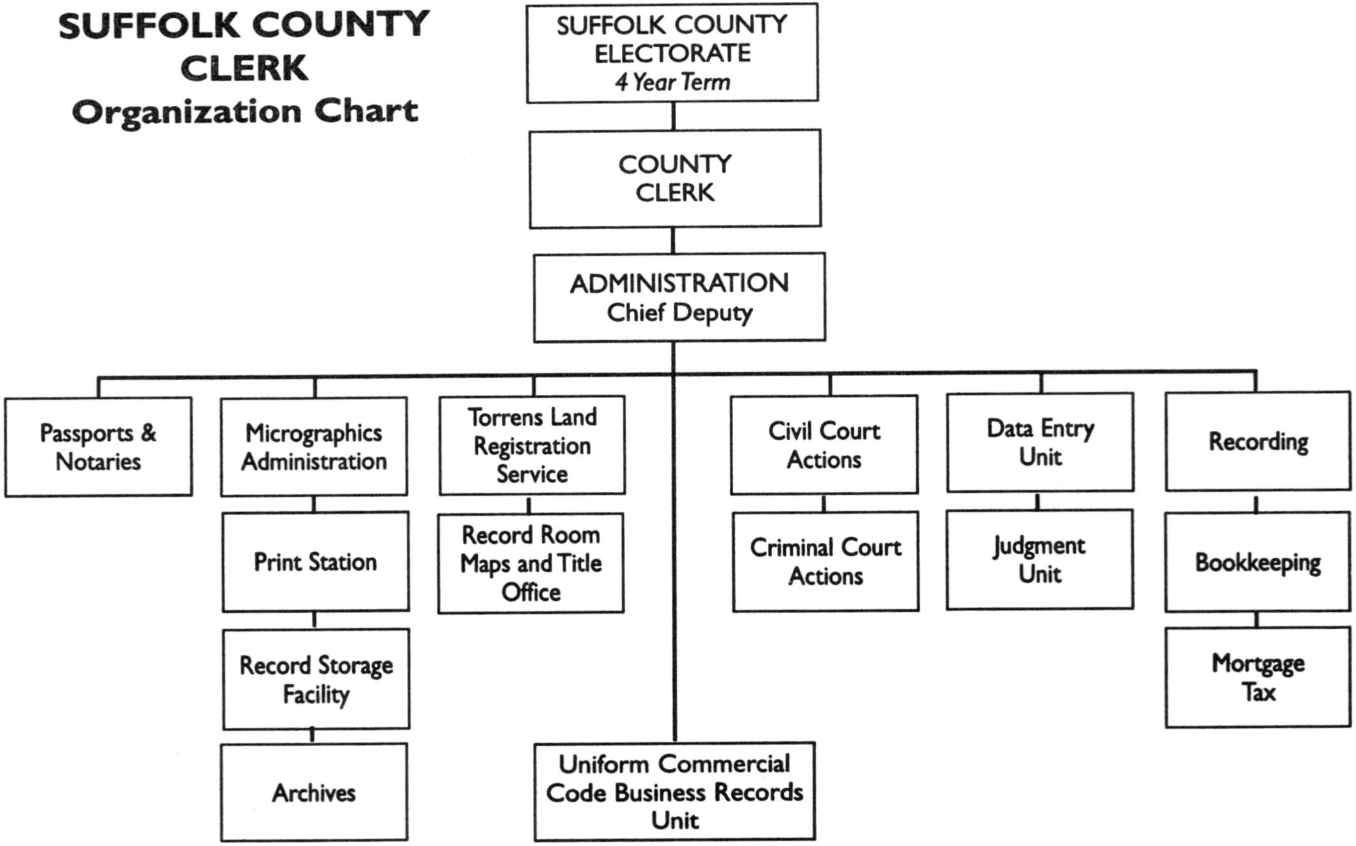

place. Why, they ask, don't the police carry out that responsibility which they do already in the County government organization? The office of sheriff has existed since the early colonial period. Only in recent times—since the middle of the 19th century—has a police department existed in County government.

The responsibilities of the County sheriff are multiple in nature.

1. (S)he acts as the LAW ENFORCEMENT officer of all decrees and mandates of the civil courts within the County. (S)he is responsible for the necessary detention of all persons accused of a crime and awaiting court action. (S)he is also responsible for the health and well-being of those committed to his/her custody following sentencing by the court. As a law enforcement officer, (s)he maintains close contact with state and federal law enforcement agencies when needed.

2. The sheriff also operates the County correctional facility. The correctional facilities are designated as follows:

    a. Maximum security. Prisoners serve time here for a serious crime, such as murder and robbery.

    b. Minimum security. Prisoners here are serving time for a less serious, or petty crime)

    c. D.W.I. facility. Persons serving a "driving while intoxicated" sentence do so here.

DEPARTMENT: SHERIFF

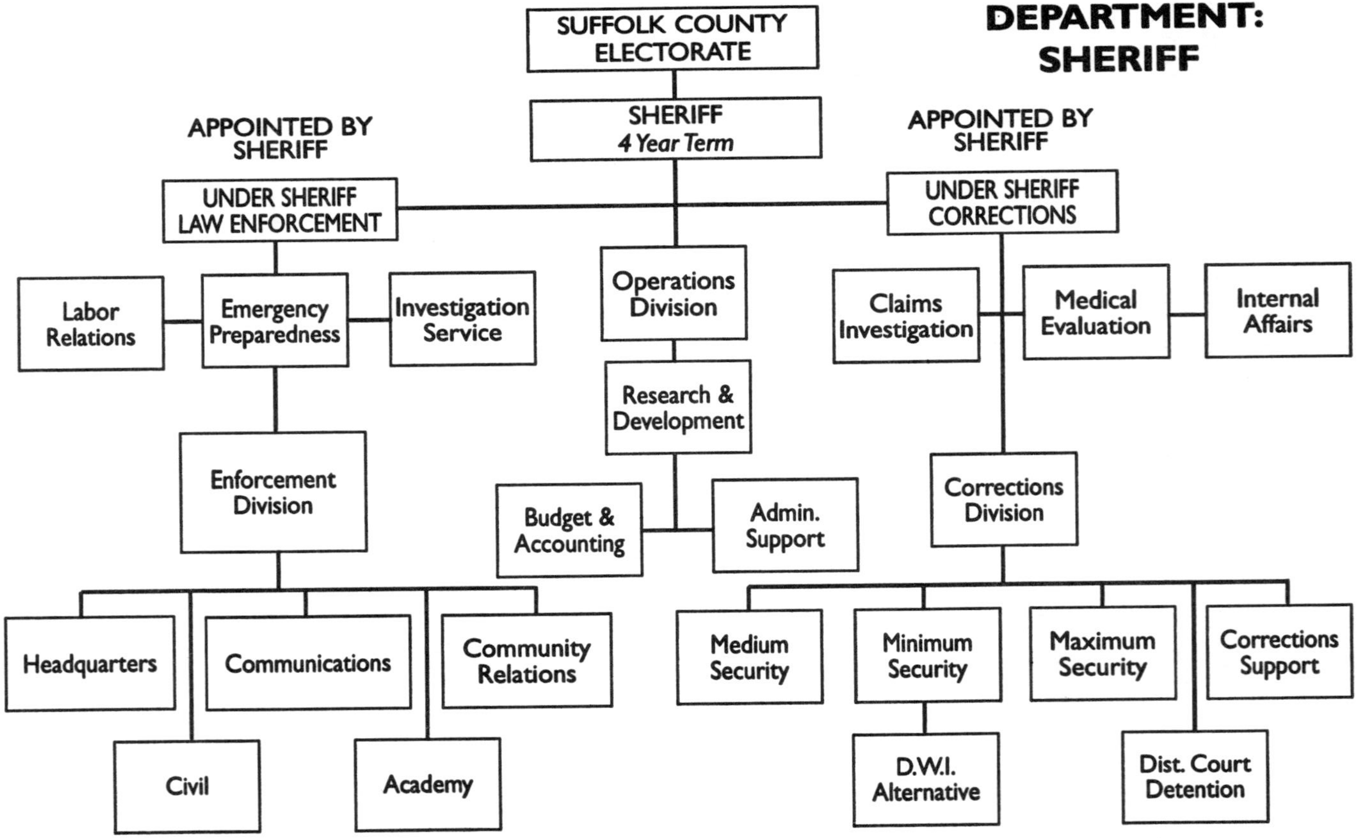

d. A facility in court where prisoners are held prior to appearing in court is likewise maintained by the County sheriff.

3. (S)he delivers prisoners to state prisons after sentencing in court.

4. The sheriff serves court papers (SUBPOENA) to citizens to appear in court as witnesses.

5. (S)he carries out court-ordered EVICTIONS of tenants who fail to pay rent to landlords.

6. (S)he can DEPUTIZE local peace officers and special deputies in natural disasters in order to protect life and property (from hurricanes, earthquakes, etc.)

7. The sheriff issues and maintains records of issued pistol licenses.

8. (S)he appoints under-sheriffs to assist him/her in carrying out his/her responsibilities.

9. (S)he supervises all correction officers (prison guards).

10. Finally, the sheriff supervises all deputy sheriffs.

The County District Attorney

The primary purpose of having a County district attorney is to PROSECUTE persons charged with committing criminal acts in the County. Examples of such crimes include murder, rape, armed robbery, drug sales, and possession of drugs. These crimes are called FELONIES. The district attorney is elected for a term of four years. (S)he is responsible for selecting a large number of ASSISTANT district attorneys to whom (s)he is authorized to assign specific criminal trials. This is obviously a very important responsibility.

Since many attorneys apply for a position as assistant district attorney, (s)he must carefully screen, interview, and check the personal background of each candidate and make wise choices. His/her record as district attorney is based on the number of CONVICTIONS his/her assistants get in the trials they prosecute in court. Most of the cases are handled by these assistants. Occasionally, a crime that has received much public attention is taken on by the district attorney himself/herself.

Bureaus of the District Attorney's Office

1. The **Case Advisory Bureau** performs initial screening and referral of felony cases. It advises all police precincts on legal matters.

2. The **Homicide Bureau** investigates and prepares for prosecution of murder trials.

3. The **District Court Bureau** provides investigation and disposition by trial or plea of misdemeanors and other offenses.

4. The **Narcotics Bureau** prosecutes individuals involved in all levels of narcotics trade.

5. The **Rackets Bureau** investigates, gathers evidence, prosecutes persons involved in organized crime in the County.

6. The **Major Crime Bureau** prosecutes the more serious and complex felony cases.

7. The **Appeals Bureau** prosecutes all cases appealed to the higher courts of the state or federal government

8. The **Family Crime Bureau** handles all juvenile crimes involving members of the same family.

9. The **Training and Education Bureau** provides additional legal education and training for prosecutors and the investigative personnel.

10. The **Environmental Crime Bureau** handles crimes dealing with public safety. It prosecutes companies that pollute the environment with hazardous waste. It also prosecutes companies that manufacture unsafe and dangerous products.

11. The **White Collar Crimes Bureau** prosecutes criminal acts of band fraud, elder abuse, tax cheating fraudulent commercial transactions, and public officials who misuse their office by taking bribes.

NOTE: A field trip to witness a court trial involving an assistant district attorney prosecuting a criminal case would be an excellent experience for the class. A guest appearance by an assistant district attorney would be a worthwhile experience.

DEPARTMENT: DISTRICT ATTORNEY

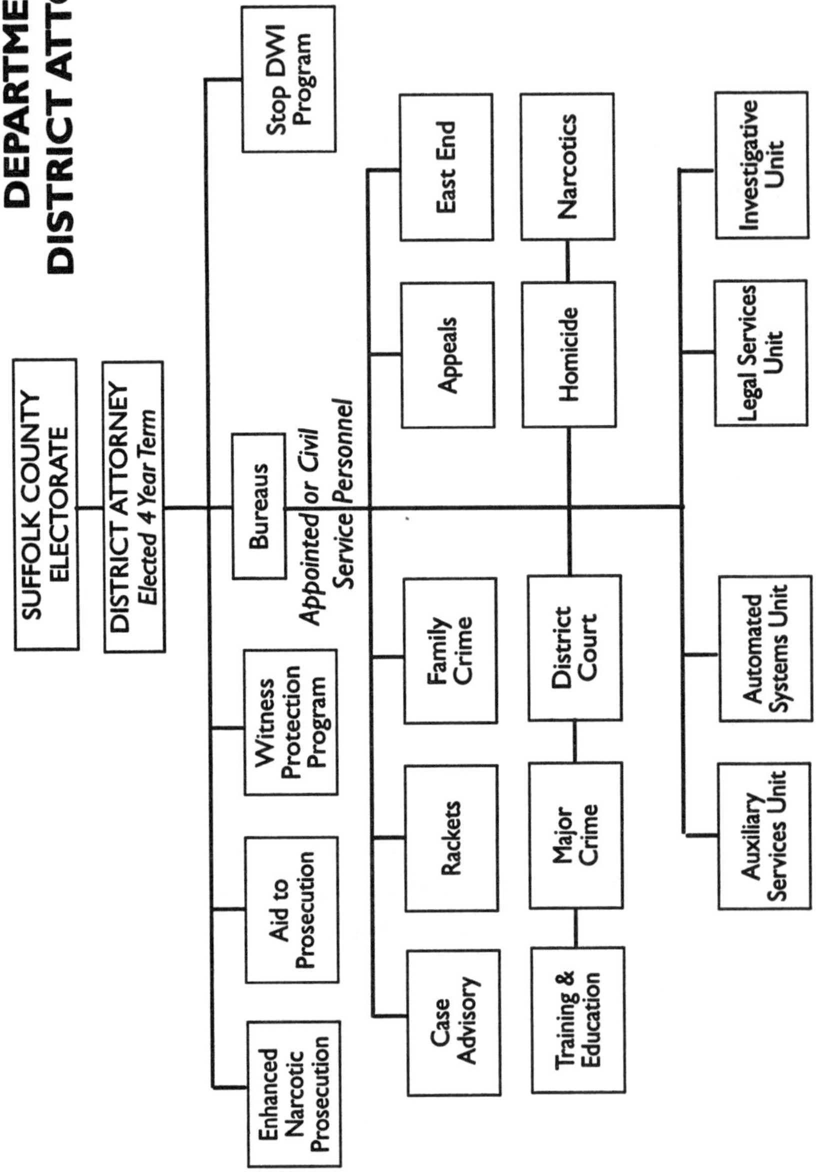

The County Executive

The County executive is the CHIEF EXECUTIVE of the County. S(he) is elected for a term of four years. (S)he has extensive power and responsibilities. The County executive is the most visible person in the County. (S)he is frequently invited to attend speaking engagements. (S)he is frequently sought after to meet with one group or another, each seeking one kind of favor or another. It is not an easy position and on any given day, (s)he will be faced with many problems that need his/her attention and decisions to take one kind of action or another.

As the growth of our population shifted to the suburban areas, the role of the County executive continued to expand as well. Today, the County executive tries to satisfy the needs of a million or more constituents.

The student should become aware of the kinds of activities that the County executive performs on a given day and the executive departments with which (s)he has day to day interaction. A student should begin to develop an appreciation for this important person and begin to realize the significant tasks carried out by this individual. A future County executive will approach this challenging position with greater awareness and preparation if (s)he is introduced to this elected official early in life. (S)he will tend to add to his/her knowledge and background of this person as (s)he matures and begins to participate actively in the political process.

The County executive must make viable choices of the many persons (s)he appoints to carry out his/her responsibilities.

(S)he must also get to know the persons who work in his/her administration as well as possible. This is very time consuming, but necessary part of the job. (S)he needs to be able to accept advice and sort out the many different kinds of advice (s)he receives and come up with good decisions. The media is always seeking him/her for interviews and picture-taking. (S)he must be able to speak well since what and how (s)he says things will be quoted in the newspapers, on TV, and radio.

Students must be made aware that being a leader requires much discipline and training and that they must develop those skills necessary to provide future leaders that will skillfully lead us in the next century. The County executive must accept the fact that his/her family time will be limited due to the long hours involved in order to perform his job well. His/her family must make some sacrifices, allowing him/her to share his/her time with others. They must be able to accept that fact that some people will be very critical of his/her performance as chief executive of the County and will express their criticisms in the press, TV and radio, and in "letters to the editor." This is part of the political process and must be understood to appreciate the complexities involved in that process.

Let us now begin to explore the responsibilities of the County executive.

The County Executive Department

There are many divisions in the County executive department. Remember that we have other County departments with ELECTED OFFICIALS (COMPTROLLER, TREASURER, CLERK, SHERIFF, AND DISTRICT ATTORNEY), each with a department of its own to administrate. The County executive must interact with these departments and exercise good judgment in asserting authority and not overstepping boundaries with these ELECTED OFFICIALS. It is a sensitive area.

The County executive APPOINTS a chief deputy executive, upon whom (s)he relies a great deal to carry out his/her important role in County government. This chief deputy helps him/her run the EXECUTIVE DEPARTMENT, which has a number of divisions. The organization chart will help the student to see the various divisions of this department. A brief discussion of each division, and the responsibilities carried out by each, will aid students' appreciation of the services performed by the people in these divisions to insure the safety and welfare of each citizen in the County.

The chief deputy executive is usually the person that helps get the County executive elected. (S)he is the person on whom the County executive relies on for important advice, and most trusts.

Divisions of the Executive Department

The chief deputy executive has the responsibility of supervising the divisions of the executive department, which follow.

1. Budget Division

This division prepares and presents the annual County budget to the County legislature for approval.

SUFFOLK COUNTY
EXECUTIVE BRANCH

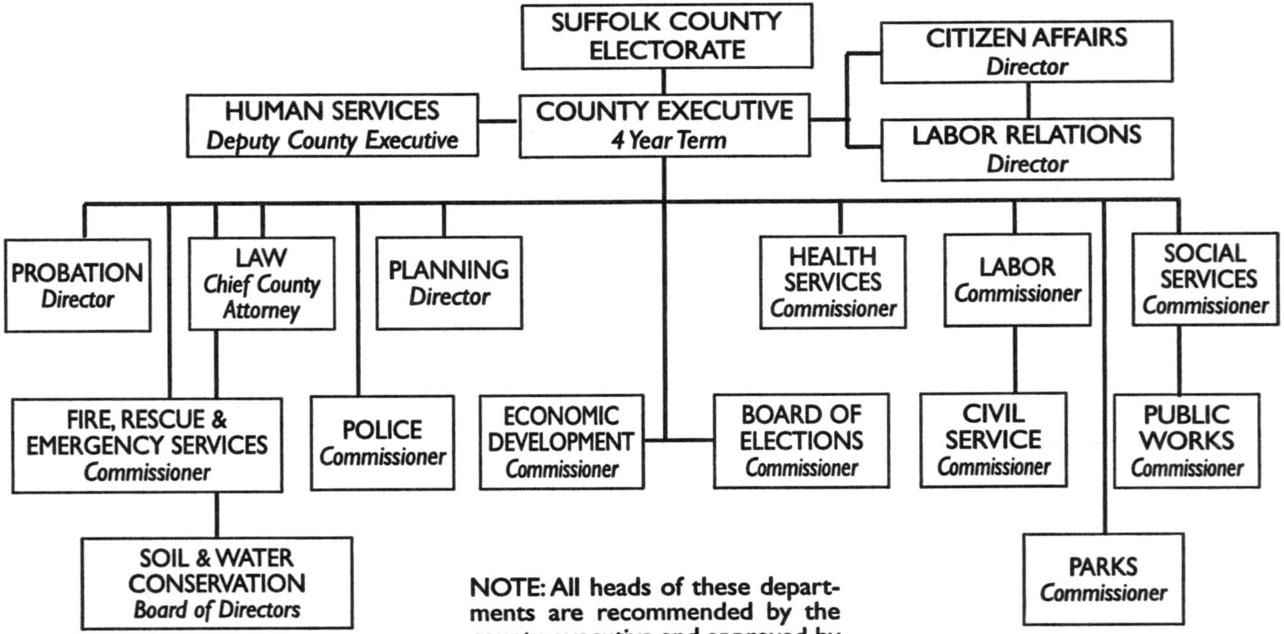

NOTE: All heads of these departments are recommended by the county executive and approved by the county legislature.

Much time goes into this activity. Well-trained accountants help to prepare this document to minimize the difficulties that goes with financial matters. The annual budget is usually submitted in the early spring for the following FISCAL year. It can take months of discussion before the budget is adopted by the County legislature.

2. Purchasing Division

This division is responsible for the purchase of all material needed to carry out the functions of ALL County operations. They try to purchase material at the most economic costs to the citizens. People submit BIDS to earn the opportunity to sell their product to the County. These competitive bids help the County to get the best price for their purchases. Accurate records are kept of these purchases.

3. Consumer Affairs Division

This division is responsible for licensing plumbers, electricians, and home improvement craftsman, as well as protecting citizens from workers who do shoddy work. They inspect gas stations and all scales used in the commercial area to insure their accuracy. In addition, they conduct public information programs to help citizens become aware of vendors who try to "rip off" consumers and have a "hot line" that can be used to ask the consumer affairs division if they have any complaints against vendors from whom they are considering buying a product.

This division carries out important functions that can save citizens from much pain and sorrow. Students are encouraged to visit this office with their parents, to utilize services to PREVENT problems from arising while using vendors with bad business practices.

4. **Human Services Division**

This is another division that plays an important role in our daily lives. It is further divided into FIVE SECTIONS.

a. Office for the aging

b. Youth bureau

c. Handicapped services

d. Veterans services

e. Office for women

These sections perform services that help each of the aforementioned groups of our population. Students should be encouraged to explore these important services, and to call up one or more of these sections for information describing their functions. Students should be encouraged to write reports on one or two of these human service sections and present them to the class.

5. **Labor Relations Division**

This division is responsible for conducting NEGOTIATIONS between County employees and County government. Most of the employees in the County acquire their position by civil service exams. They receive a salary based on the negotiations that take place when labor contracts expire. Labor and management personnel then sit at the BARGAINING TABLE and try to arrive at a fair and equitable contract.

A County can have as many as 5000 employees. Each department and division in the County contains a number of employees who work under a contract agreement reached between the County and union leaders.

6. **Stop-DWI Traffic Programs**

This division, new to the County government, maintains an ongoing program to alert the public regarding the dangers involved in operating a motor vehicle while under the influence of alcohol. The sad statistics are that too many people, especially the younger drivers, are seriously hurt and killed due to road accidents caused by DWI drivers. Students should be encouraged to write a letter to this division asking for information about their important role in County government. A guest speaker from this division would also be a relevant activity for the students to experience.

7. **Intergovernmental Relations Division**

This division conducts ongoing dialogue with elected officials in federal, state, and town government. This exchange is necessary for creating harmonious relationships with these governmental officials. The County executive has to articulate the needs of the County to gain financial assistance from state and federal government. (S)he may visit Congress and speak before a particular committee regarding financial assistance from the federal government to carry out needed services for the citizens of the County. The same can happen at the state legislature level, where the County executive speaks before a state assembly or state senate committee hearing.

The personnel in this division keep up an ongoing communication with important people in the state and federal government so that the County executive is continually apprised of affairs. When (s)he does appear before legislatures or department officials, federal or state, (s)he has been briefed as to what to say. Knowledgeable people are so necessary in this division to help the County executive interact well with state and federal government.

8. **Minority Affairs Division**

This division helps to maintain harmonious relations with County citizens of minority background. All types of discrimination, including racial and religious, are dealt with as soon as possible to keep the community free of problems that can result in divided communities. Well-trained people in interpersonal relations are needed in this very important division of County government.

9. **Telecommunications Division**

This division is responsible for maintaining at peak performance all means of communications within the County. Good communication is an important part of running a County government with efficiency. During emergencies, such as hurricanes and other natural disasters, the breakdown of communications must be quickly restored. County employees depend heavily on this department to keep the public informed on what to do during these periods.

Personnel in this department conduct ongoing training programs to help county employees deal with unexpected disasters. Many lives can be lost if the communications systems fail to be maintained during natural disasters.

10. **Community Development Agency**

It is a known fact that when a community begins to show signs of physical decay, a general atmosphere of unrest develops among the residents, leading to neighborhood disputes, an increase in drug sales and usage, and a higher crime rate.

This relatively new section of the executive department is specifically charged with developing projects to improve community facilities designed primarily for persons of low to moderate incomes. It is also delegated to prevent or eliminate areas of blight (slums) within our communities.

Specifically, the community development agency carries out the following activities designed to meet urgent needs:

a. Seeking federal government funds to help those in need of moderate and low cost housing.

b. Holding periodic public hearings to make citizens aware of their services to locate families needing low cost and moderate housing.

c. Furnishing counseling services to help people seek banking loans necessary to purchase low cost or moderate cost housing.

d. Providing low cost loans to qualified County citizens to purchase moderate or low cost homes.

e. Giving emergency shelter grants for those in need of immediate temporary housing (the homeless).

This agency is managed by an appointed director selected by the County executive and approved by the County legislature.

Last but certainly not least, SUPPORT PERSONNEL are needed in order to operate the executive department (as well as other governmental departments). These people are trained, highly efficient in making sure that the County executive is available as much as possible to serve his/her constituents.

In particular, support personnel prepare important papers for public notices, arrange appointments, and schedule the time of the executive and other department heads. They answer the telephone, respond to requests from citizens to see the County executive, and greet people when they visit. They also arrange press conferences and television appearances in advance.

When the County executive travels, (s)he is always accompanied by a small group of trusted aides who help him/her get to where (s)he has to go, keeping problems to a minimum. (S)he is usually driven to and from public

DEPARTMENT: COMMUNITY DEVELOPMENT

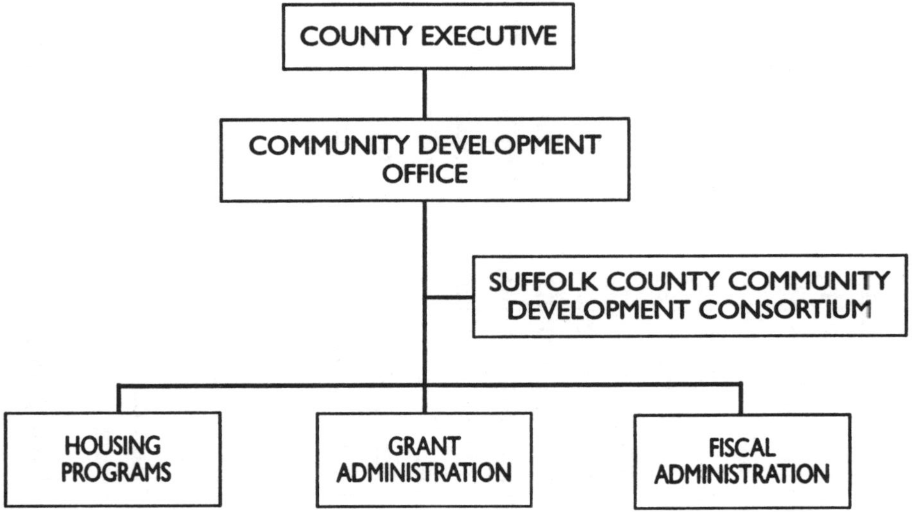

appearances, and has a personal bodyguard for protection from possible danger from a discontented citizen.

All kinds of precautions are taken to prevent the County executive from being exposed to a dangerous situation. Most of the people who serve the County executive in this manner are well known by him/her. Often these are the people s(he) will also socialize with, since there is a need for constant communication with personal staff members in order to fulfill the daily demands made by citizens for his/her personal attention. The success or failure of a County executive hinges on how well his support staff performs.

The County executive, as we just read, administers the executive department. This department is physically located near his/her office. (S)he can, if (s)he wishes, walk to these office locations and talk with the personnel in that office. (S)he usually holds weekly meetings with the heads of the preceding divisions in the executive department, and keeps up with everything (s)he needs to be on top of.

In addition to this very important department, there are a number of other departments that render important services to citizens of the County.

The Health Services Department

This department is administered by a health commissioner, and carries out the following.

1. It safeguards and improves the general health of the people living in the County.

2. It conducts preventative health services (immunization programs).

3. It conducts a continuing health education program aimed at helping:

    a. Young mothers

    b. Senior citizens

    c. Disabled citizens

4. It administers an alcohol and substance abuse treatment program.

5. It oversees the reporting and the control of infectious and contagious diseases.

6. It provides home health services to persons who are housebound.

7. It provides nursing care, physical therapy, and speech therapy to those who otherwise could not afford these services.

8. It provides health related services to eligible pre-school disabled children to help them get a more successful start when they enter kindergarten class.

9. It inspects restaurants to insure that food is handled by healthy workers (and that they maintain sanitary conditions by proper handwashing) and that food is kept properly refrigerated.

DEPARTMENT: HEALTH SERVICES

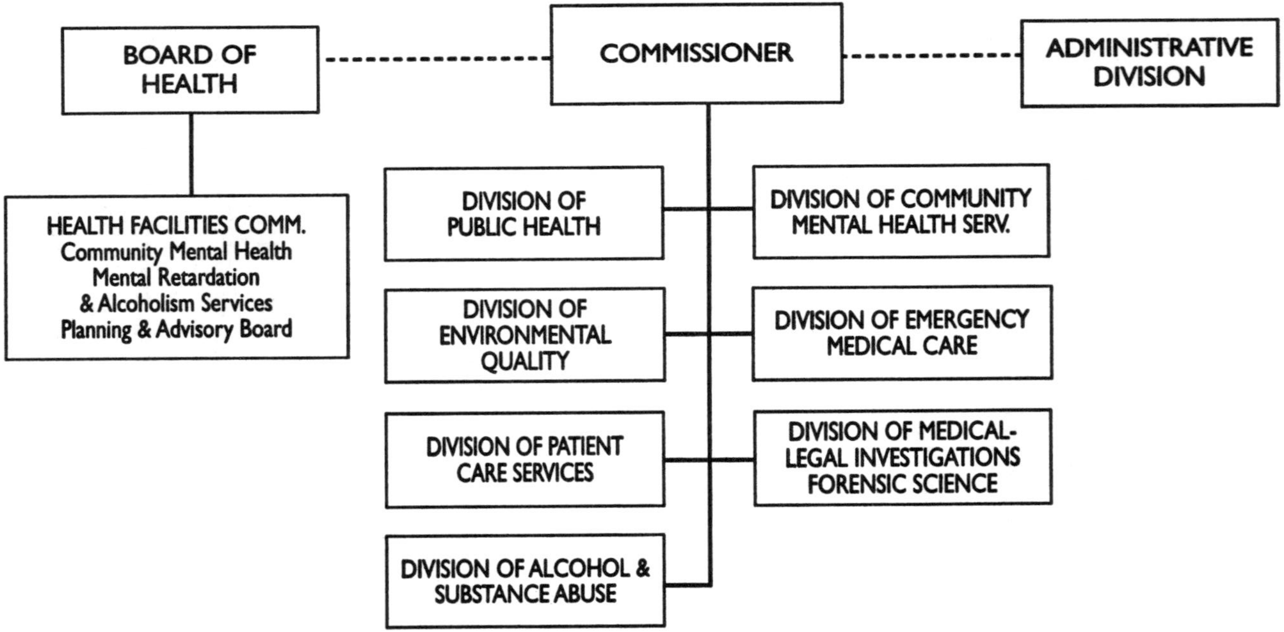

10. It inspects public places—amusement centers, movie theaters, etc.—to insure that the facilities are kept in sanitary condition.

11. It provides pre-natal medical attention for mothers who cannot afford these services.

12. It provides medical attention to prisoners serving their sentence in County correctional institutions.

13. It operates health stations where citizens who cannot afford medical services can receive proper medical attention.

14. It operates an **Environmental Quality Division**, which is responsible for monitoring:

    a. Air quality

    b. Water supply

    c. Solid waste disposal

    d. Industrial waste disposal

    e. Sewage treatment facilities

15. It operates an office of ecology that monitors and conducts ongoing tests, protecting our marine life environment, inland fresh water, open spaces, and wetlands.

16. It operates medical laboratories with health services for police, district attorney and probation departments.

17. It assists emergency medical service personnel by providing mobile radios, advanced medical equipment to emergency vehicles. It also designates qualified hospitals and physicians.

18. It maintains a close relationship with department of fire, rescue and emergency services and provides counseling services for members of these departments.

19. It runs the **Medical-Legal Investigations and Forensic Sciences Division**, which investigates sudden, suspicious, accidental or unattended deaths by conducting a scientific investigation of the manner and cause of death, reporting the findings to the public and courts. It also provides chemical testing of urine samples from probationers and the patients of methadone clinics to detect the presence of drugs.

20. It provides community mental health services to the mentally ill and mentally retarded.

NOTE: the teacher should not attempt to have students memorize these services, but should encourage students to realize and appreciate how many important services are provided by this single County department. A discussion should be facilitated by asking students to share any personal experiences they have had that relate to any of the services that have been outlined above. The teacher can also assign students to ask their parents about any experiences they have had that relate to the health services department.

Glossary terms include: 1) retarded 2) forensic 3) pre-natal 4) sanitary 5) contagious 6) ecology 7) monitor 8) environment.

The Social Services Department

The role of this vital County department is to provide needed services for the many people who may require immediate attention. At one time or another, many citizens living in the County need to contact this department for emergency services. For example, a family member, who is the main provider of the family, loses his/her job and suddenly there is a serious financial crisis.

These kinds of serious needs and many others are dealt with by the people who work in this department. Therefore trained persons are necessary, who can sensitively deal with people applying for assistance for which they would rather not apply.

The person who initiates the process of applying for public assistance is a CASE WORKER. (S)he conducts the interview to complete the APPLICATION that the person needing assistance needs to fill out. The case worker needs to ask many personal questions that can make the APPLICANT uncomfortable, somewhat embarrassed and angry, simultaneously. That is why well-trained persons need to be involved in this process.

Although they make up only a small percentage when compared to those who really need assistance, there are at times people who may not deserve the help. These people are called WELFARE CHEATS. Some would even apply for TWO checks, or more.

Thus, the social services department was recently ordered to FINGERPRINT all applicants. There was a great debate over this decision, but the FINGERPRINTING requirement became part of applying for public assistance. Because of the humility people experience in going through the process of being fingerprinted and answering all those personal questions, some eligible for public assistance no longer apply.

The department provides other services:

1. It provides child protection services. A hot line is available for persons to call if they know of any child being abused by a parent, or any other person that deals with the child. This has been in effect since 1973. Since that time, over one million referrals have been made to the New York State hot line to report possible child abuse. The law mandates (orders) the County social services department to respond within twenty-four hours and investigate the ALLEGATIONS (accusations).

2. It provides foster care for children who need to be relocated from their family because of illness of parent or the incompetence of the parent(s) to take care of their children. SOCIAL WORKERS from the department interview prospective foster parents to see if they are fit to take care of the children in their charge.

3. It operates day care centers for working mothers who cannot afford regular day care expenses. The center is operated by well-trained persons who teach the children and feed the children nutritious meals.

4. It administrates ADOPTION SERVICES to place orphaned children or unwanted children in homes where

they will assuredly receive proper upbringing. Periodic visits are made to homes of adoptive parents to see how things are going for the child.

5. It offers a variety of employment and employment-related training services so persons getting assistance can develop job skills that will fetch a better paying job, taking them off public assistance.

6. An emergency assistance program helps households with expenses such as fuel bills, house repairs, utilities, food, and other essential needs.

7. MEDICAID services are provided for eligible receivers of public assistance. This includes paying for medical expenses, eye glasses, dentist visits, prescriptions for drugs, nursing care, and hospital stays.

8. The FOOD STAMP PROGRAM distributes allotments to families receiving assistance to make purchases of certain food commodities and assure the family of adequate food supplies. Supermarkets and other food-selling stores accept these stamps (coupons).

9. It provides medical transportation to eligible Medicaid receivers to make visits to health service providers.

10. It helps persons on public assistance to find adequate housing when necessary.

11. Counseling services assist families in preventing a child at risk from entering foster care.

DEPARTMENT: SOCIAL SERVICES

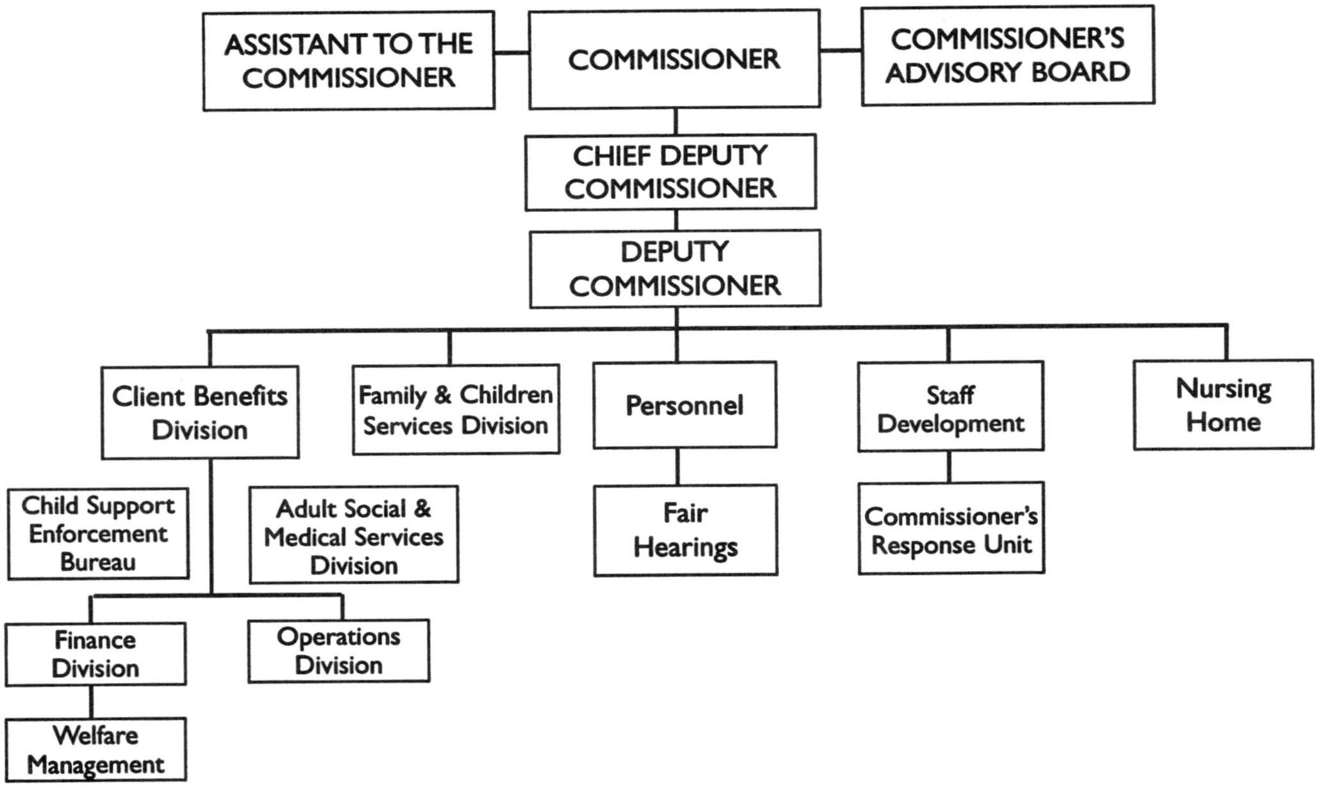

12. It protects those who are physically/mentally impaired from being abused by others and harmed by themselves.

The social services department is administered by a commissioner, chief deputy commissioner and a deputy commissioner. All three are APPOINTED.

NOTE: A guest appearance by a social services department social worker or case worker would be very worthwhile for the children during the study of this department. Children should prepare ten to fifteen questions ready to pose the guest speaker. Also, most relevant material can be available for the teacher to share with the class by writing the social services department.

The Public Works Department

The public works commissioner administers the important County public works department. (S)he is APPOINTED by the County executive and approved by the County legislature. The public works commissioner must have a background in mechanical engineering. (S)he must also be knowledgeable about road construction, bridges, and supervising persons working under his/her command.

A large part of the County government budget is spent by this department. County roads must be kept properly maintained so that citizens can experience safe traveling when using them. During winter months, roads must be kept free of snow and ice which create dangerous driving conditions. Bridges must be well constructed to handle the traffic that crosses them. Bridges must be periodically examined for any structural damage that could create a serious catastrophe.

The role of the public works department is to carry out the following responsibilities:

1. It designs buildings owned, rented, and operated by the County.

2. It constructs and maintains all roads, sidewalks, canals, locks, channels, bridges, docks, marinas, beach erosion projects, drainage structures operated by the County government.

3. It is responsible for moving any County offices that change location.

4. It surveys property acquired for County use. This is done by the engineering staff.

5. It conducts ongoing tests of construction material used for roads (asphalt, concrete, etc.) buildings and sewer projects. They are always concerned about SAFETY of those using County buildings, and other County facilities.

6. The department oversees snow removal and sanding of icy roads in the winter.

7. It plans, builds, and maintains parking lots used by citizens to conduct business with County personnel.

8. It furnishes security and custodial services to all County and court facilities.

DEPARTMENT: PUBLIC WORKS

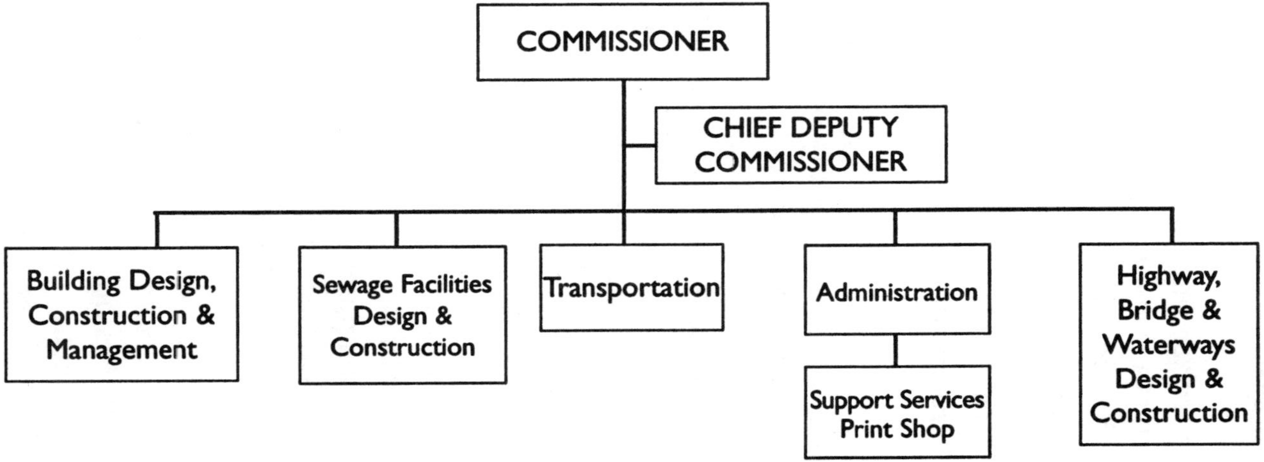

9. It provides transportation planning for the County transit system.

10. It supervises and inspects the dredging of waterways by private contractors. Periodic dredging is done to keep channels deep enough for boats to pass in safety to open water.

11. It is responsible for the control of the mosquito population throughout the County.

12. It maintains a truck garage to make regular mechanical inspection of all County-owned vehicles and other road-building equipment.

This department employs several hundred civil service workers. They are represented by a union and work under a collective-bargaining contract.

The County Law Department

The COUNTY ATTORNEY is the chief administrator of the law department. (S)he is APPOINTED by the County executive and approved by the County legislature. This department carries out many functions that help the County government carry out their responsibilities.

In addition to the County attorney, there are three other attorneys that serve under him/her as deputies. These deputy attorneys help supervise the numerous divisions in this department. These deputy attorneys are also APPOINTED, after being recommended by the County attorney, and approved by the County executive.

NOTE: A review of the organizational chart would help give students a broad picture of the various activities carried out by this department. The teacher could use this department to initiate a discussion about diversified careers available in law.

The law department carries out the following:

1. Handling all the legal business of the County and its agencies.

2. Prosecuting and defending all civil actions and proceedings brought by or against the County, the County legislature, and any officer whose salary is paid for from County funds for an official act.

3. Prosecuting all juvenile delinquency petitions, child-abuse and neglect petitions, termination of parental rights, and review of foster care petitions.

4. The County attorney is charged with representing the **Child-Support Enforcement Bureau** in the enforcement of child support and spousal (father) support obligations.

5. Investigating alleged discrimination on the basis of race, color, creed, age, sex, national origin, disability, marital status; helping foster mutual respect and understanding among all racial, religious, and nationality groups in the community.

6. Educating County residents about incidents of discrimination.

7. Distributing information emphasizing prevention of discrimination to institutions such as schools and workplace.

8. Providing services of mediation, arbitration, and consultation, which helps to resolve problems before they arise and become serious.

9. The **Division of Real Estate** buys, maintains, as well as disposes, of all County real estate property. Also, it generates revenue (money) through the sale of surplus County property at auction.

10. Offering legal advice to all County agencies, boards, commissions, departments, and panels regarding their activities and responsibilities.

11. Reviewing, revising and approving written agreements and documents pertaining to the borrowing of money.

12. Assisting the County legislature, County executive and all other County agencies with regards to legislative matters and questions of law.

13. Acquiring property for all the County's land projects (example: farmland acquisition, Open Space program).

14. Generating revenue by sale of surplus County property at auction, and direct sale to adjoining owners.

15. Appointed County attorneys also help the County executive run his/her election campaign and take leaves of absence during the campaign period to help the

County Executive get re-elected and thus assure their continuing work in the law department. This aspect of the political process should be discussed by the class and the pros and cons of this phenomenon should be examined and understood by the students.

NOTE: The teacher would find it very beneficial to invite a member of the law department to visit the students. Suggested questions to ask the visiting County attorney are available and should be distributed to the class for them to ask the visiting attorney. The purpose of studying this department is to help students grasp the considerable influence of lawyers in our government and the specific duties they carry out, enabling our government to function efficiently. Again, students need not memorize, but use the listed duties to as a means of facilitating discussion.

The County Labor Department

This department was established to prevent and resolve labor disputes that could effect the economy of the County. It also administers various employment and training programs designed to help unemployed workers to acquire new skills to find a new job. The chief administrator is the labor commissioner. (S)he is APPOINTED by the County executive and approved by the County legislature.

The role of this department is displayed in the activities inscribed below:

1. Compiling, interpreting, and distributing labor statistics for the business community and interested residents.

2. Providing trained and qualified mediators to help settle difficult labor disputes.

3. Training and certifying labor mediators and arbitrators.

4. Certifying all County employee collective-bargaining units.

5. Assigning individuals receiving public assistance to jobs that will train them for future employment opportunities.

DEPARTMENT: LABOR

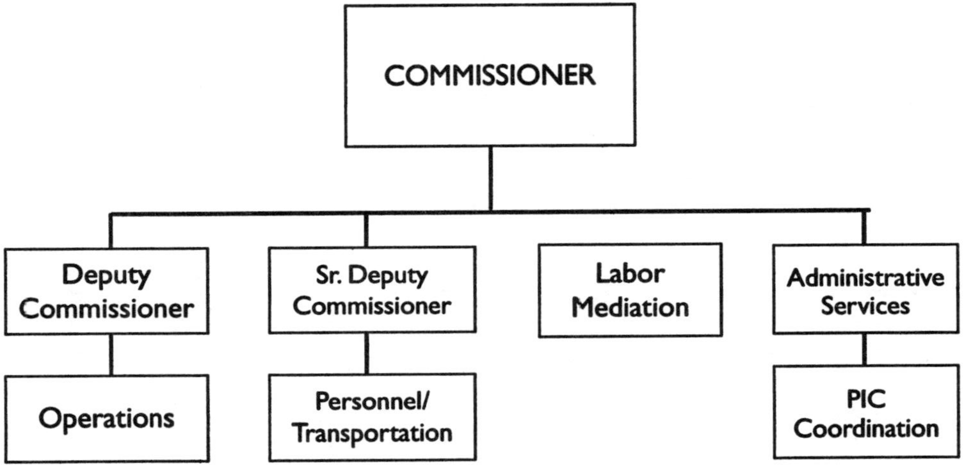

QUESTIONS TO ASK GUEST SPEAKER FROM OFFICE OF THE SUFFOLK COUNTY ATTORNEY'S OFFICE

1. What made you decide to become an attorney?

2. Were you always a County attorney? If not, what kind of legal cases did you try before you became a County attorney?

3. How long have you served as a County attorney?

4. What are your responsibilities as a County attorney?

5. What advice could you give us to become more politically astute?

6. How did you get involved in politics?

7. How do you get to become a County attorney?

8. How many attorneys work in your office?

9. What interesting cases have you been involved in during your time as County attorney?

10. What advice can you give us as students to become attorneys?

11 What political party do you belong to?

12. What made you decide to join that political party?

13. What are some of the problems we young citizens need to help solve in the future years in Suffolk County?

14. Why is it important to become politically astute?

15. What are your future plans in government?

The County Police Department

All young students are aware of the existence of a police department. They are familiar with the role of police as protectors of the community. On a daily basis, they see policemen on patrol in police squad cars or motorcycles.

However, they are not as familiar with the unseen activities that take place in police headquarters and in police laboratories that help solve crimes. Nor are they aware of the painstaking work done at the scene of a crime or accident to try to detect the background of a crime or the cause of an accident.

The teacher should motivate the students to pique their interest to more fully understand the extensive responsibilities of law enforcement personnel. Detectives assigned to criminal investigations can become very discouraged when a criminal case remains unsolved after following many leads or clues for weeks on end. Students need to understand that many criminal acts go unsolved. Attitudes of students toward police officers should be discussed during this study. Discussions of this nature serve to develop a fairer, and more positive, image of the personnel assigned to insuring the safety and security of citizens in a community.

The primary mission of the County police department is to preserve the public peace, prevent crime, detect and arrest offenders, protect the rights of persons and property, and enforce all laws in the County. The County police department is divided into two major divisions.

1. **Headquarters**. This division offers comprehensive and specialized services to all law enforcement agencies within the County including town and village police units. Services include:

    a. Police laboratories

    b. Chemists, fingerprint experts, lab technicians, and criminologists

2. **Police Districts**. The County police department is divided into geographical units called PRECINCTS.

    a. These precincts are staffed by various personnel that include:

        (1) Police captain

        (2) Police lieutenant

        (3) Police sergeant

        (4) Squad car officers

        (5) Foot officers

    b. In addition a precinct contains a detective office. Detectives conduct investigations from this office and are assigned their cases by the chief of detectives. They utilize the facilities and services offered by the headquarters division. The types of cases that detectives investigate include:

COUNTY POLICE DEPARTMENT ORGANIZATION

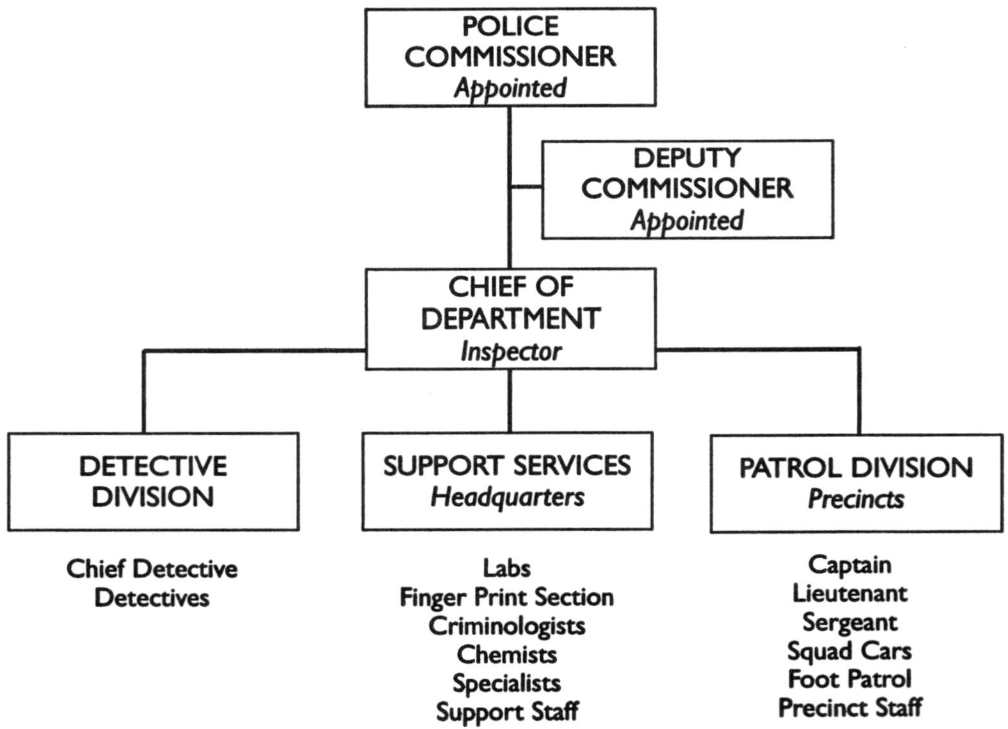

(1) Murder

(2) Robbery

(3) Felonies

(4) Misdemeanors

(5) Rapes

(6) Drug sales and use of drugs

(7) Larcenies

(8) Harassment

(9) Physical abuse cases

The County Board of Elections

The board of elections is a BIPARTISAN body established to administer, supervise, and conduct ALL primary and general elections in the County. The board of elections is responsible to instill confidence in the electoral system, something that is fundamental to the integrity of the democratic process. The activities and responsibilities of the board are meant to assure county citizens that fair and accurate elections are being held and that those who try to commit election fraud will be punished quickly and severely. Specifically, the responsibilities of the County board of elections are to:

1. SUPERVISE and OPERATE all elections held in the County, as authorized by New York State Election Law. These include:

    a. General elections, held in November.

    b. General primaries, held in September.

    c. Presidential primaries, held in April.

    d. Village elections, held in March or April.

    e. Fire commissioner elections, held at various times of the year.

    f. Library elections (trustees, budgets), held at various times of the year.

    g. School district elections, held in May.

    h. Special elections, held whenever someone resigns or dies while in office.

2. Conduct REGISTRATION DRIVES and encourage citizens to register to be able to VOTE.

3. Maintain accurate records of registered voters.

4. Assign ELECTION INSPECTORS and POLL WATCHERS on ALL election days to supervise the polling places and prevent elections fraud from occurring.

5. Notify voters of coming elections informing voters where they should go to cast their ballots.

6. Conduct the ABSENTEE BALLOT program to assist voters who may not be able to get to polling place on election day.

7. CERTIFY DESIGNATING PETITIONS of candidates wishing to run for political office.

8. CERTIFY candidates who win the elections and officially notify them.

9. IMPOUND voting machines to make sure that an accurate vote count is made.

10. Maintain all voting machines in proper operating order.

11. Issue media releases to inform public of winning candidates.

12. Designate where polling places will be located and assign necessary voting machines to each polling place.

COUNTY BOARD OF ELECTIONS

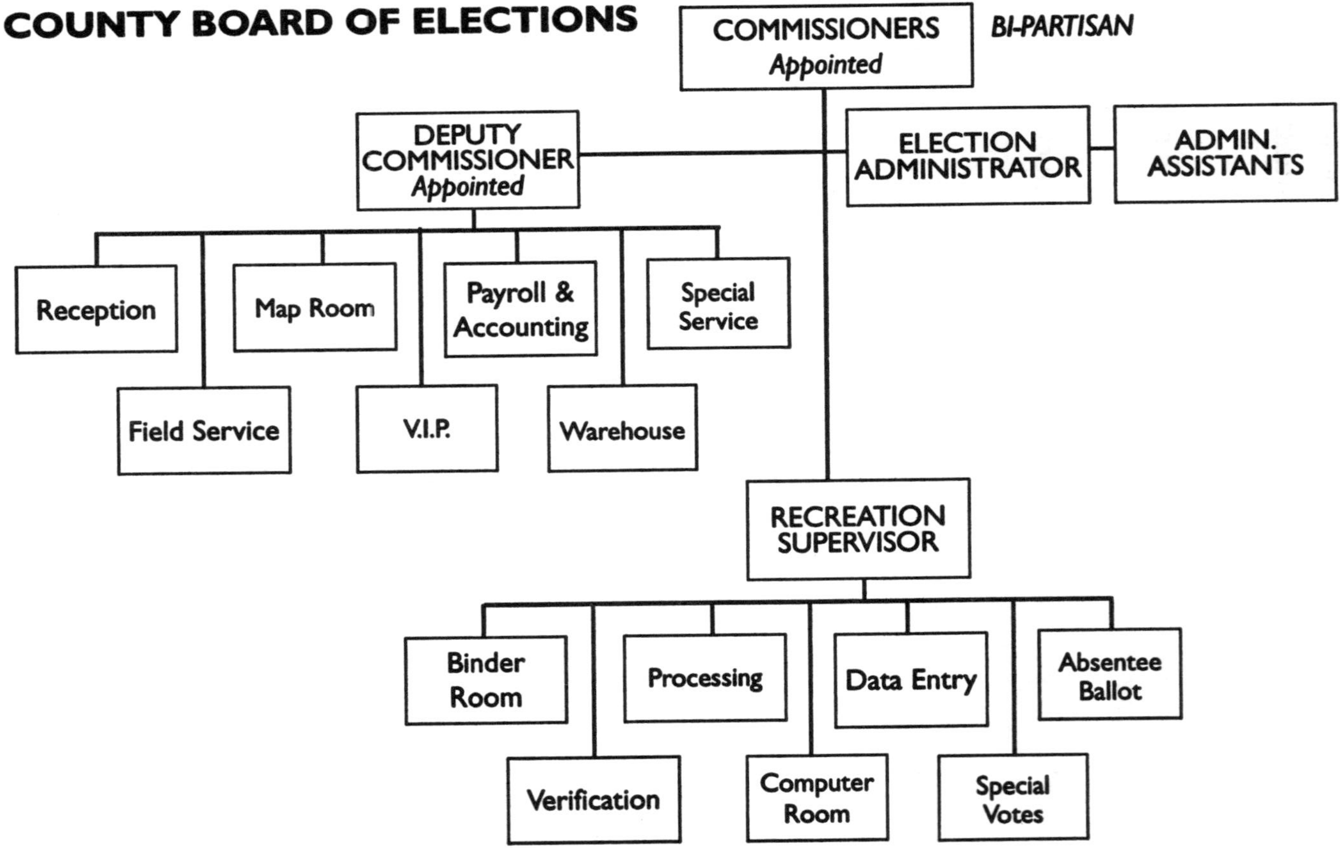

SUGGESTED QUESTIONS TO ASK BOARD OF ELECTIONS COMMISSIONERS DURING BOARD OF ELECTIONS FIELD TRIP

1. How do board of elections commissioners acquire their positions?

2. How many persons work in the board of elections?

3. How do they acquire their position?

4. How does the board of elections go about determining how the candidates get on the ballot?

5. What is a DESIGNATING PETITION?

6. How is it determined which party gets on row A, B, C, etc.?

7. What happens if a voting machine fails to operate?

8. Why are more voters choosing to register INDEPENDENT instead of choosing a particular party affiliation?

9. Does a voter have to vote every year to remain registered?

10. Why is it important to register in a particular party designation?

11. How can I become a poll worker?

12. How can I become a party worker?

13. Do you like your job? Why?

14. What advice can you give us to become more politically astute?

15. What are your responsibilities as an elections commissioner?

16. What are some improvements you would like to see in the voting process that would encourage more citizens to participate in the political process?

17. Are more citizens voting these days or less?

18. What would I have to do to run for public office?

19. What role do the County leaders play in the selection of candidates for political office?

20. What does CROSS-ENDORSEMENT mean?

21. What role do the town leaders play in the selection of candidates for public office?

22. What is a primary? Are they important in the political process?

The County Parks Department

Established to maintain all County parks for public use, the County parks department is authorized to recommend programs to preserve the natural resources, greenery, wildlife and the habitats of fish, birds, and animals in the County. It meets regularly with interested nature-loving organizations as part of its responsibility to organize activities and develop facilities and programs for the citizens of the County. The parks department provides guided tours of its park facilities, nature walks, and bicycle trails.

Trained park police help citizens enjoy the parks in safety. It also has increased programs for the handicapped to make better use of park facilities. An ongoing education program is conducted by park personnel to help insure that parks will be safe for use and preserve the natural habitat for future generations. An appointed parks commissioner administers the department. Most park personnel are civil service employees who acquire their position by taking a competitive examination. Parks department administrators train park employees to help them serve the needs of the parks' users as efficiently as possible. As populations of a County increase, the County administrators make every effort to increase parks' area by acquiring more property for use as parks.

Recreational activities play an important part in the daily life of citizens. Students should be made aware that parks must be used wisely. Carelessness on the part of citizens results in deterioration of parks and large expenditures of money to restore them. This results in higher tax rates. Teacher should facilitate a discussion on the importance of

DEPARTMENT: PARKS

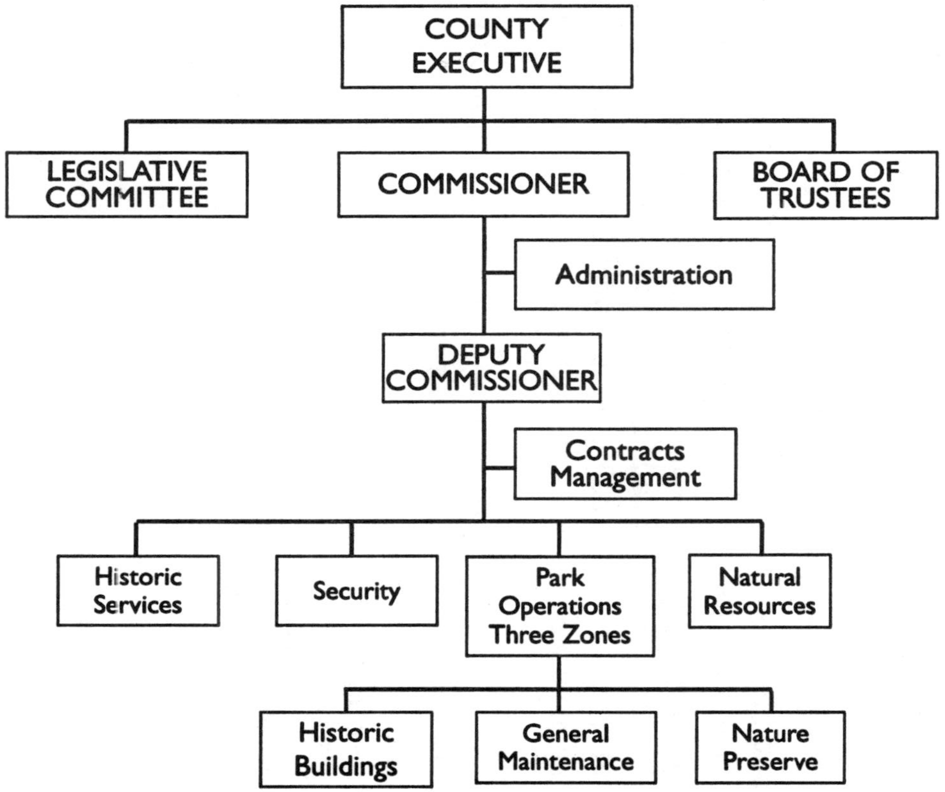

preserving our open spaces, stressing that the potential result of carelessness on the part of citizens is that they will have no parks to use for their enjoyment. Hence, some parks need to charge fees for their use. Money collected is used solely to help maintain the park facilities.

The Civil Services/Human Resources Department

This department provides and administers competitive examinations for positions in County, towns, villages, school and other special districts. It maintains test score lists of job classifications, from which names are taken for open job positions. It advertises, in the medical field, where and when tests are being administered. Test lists are publicly displayed on bulletin boards of the civil service office.

The civil service fulfills a crucial responsibility by attracting the best qualified persons for vacancies in government positions. Most persons working for all levels of government (village, town, county, etc.) are CIVIL SERVICE EMPLOYEES. This department is likewise administered by an APPOINTED commissioner, recommended by the County executive, and approved by the County legislature.

The Economic Development Department

Economics plays a very important part in the lives of citizens. If businesses fail, people lose jobs. If people lose jobs, people can't pay taxes on their property and need

DEPARTMENT: CIVIL SERVICE/HUMAN SERVICE

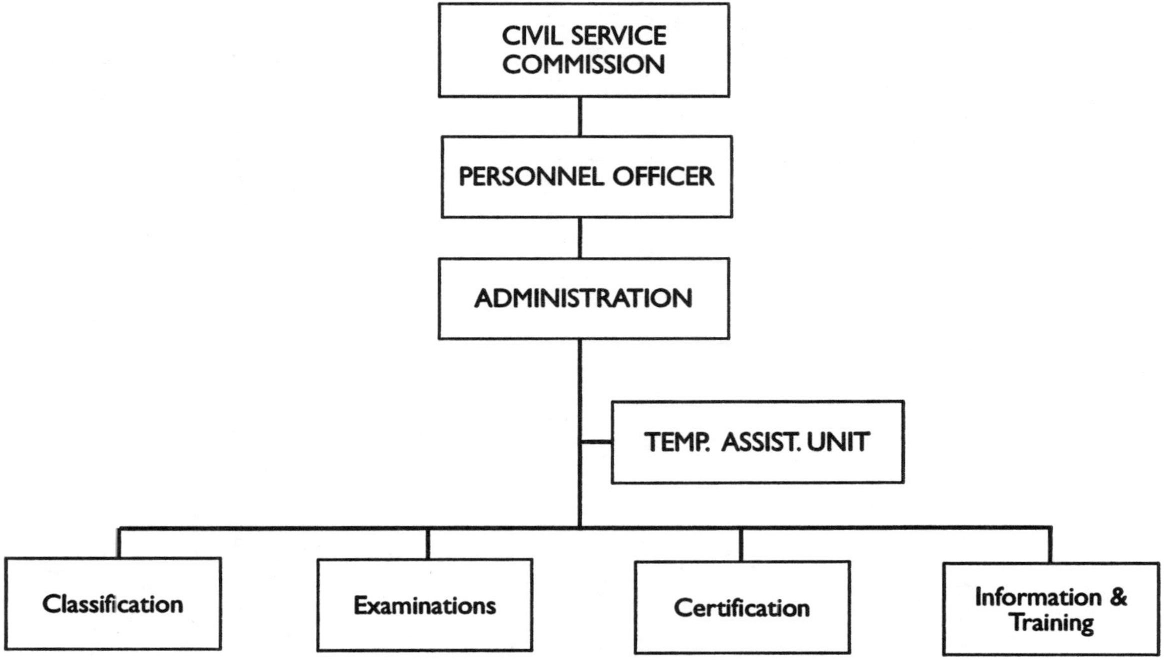

public assistance. Business failure also results in those businesses not paying their corporation taxes and further reduces the money coming into the County treasury.

This department provides assistance to industries and business establishments to help them financially succeed. Economic development staff try to keep a close relationship with business leaders. The Long Island Business Association is a well-organized group of business leaders. They meet on a monthly basis and discuss how things are going economically in the County. Are taxes going up? Are the cost of public utilities (gas, electric, water) increasing? Businesses and corporations are constantly approached to locate their operations in another area. The competition is fierce. Other locales send representatives to these companies to offer them "DEALS" that might make them consider re-locating.

The County economic development department tries to look for ways to help make businesses and corporations earn good profits from their investment of time, talent, and money. This department is authorized to provide loans to qualified companies as an incentive for them to operate their company in the County. It also provides trained advisors to companies who may want to DIVERSIFY (expand, widen) their operations. An industrial development agency is part of this department. It makes every effort to attract new industry to the County's economy. The department uses varied media to attract out-of-County companies to relocate in the County.

DEPARTMENT: ECONOMIC DEVELOPMENT

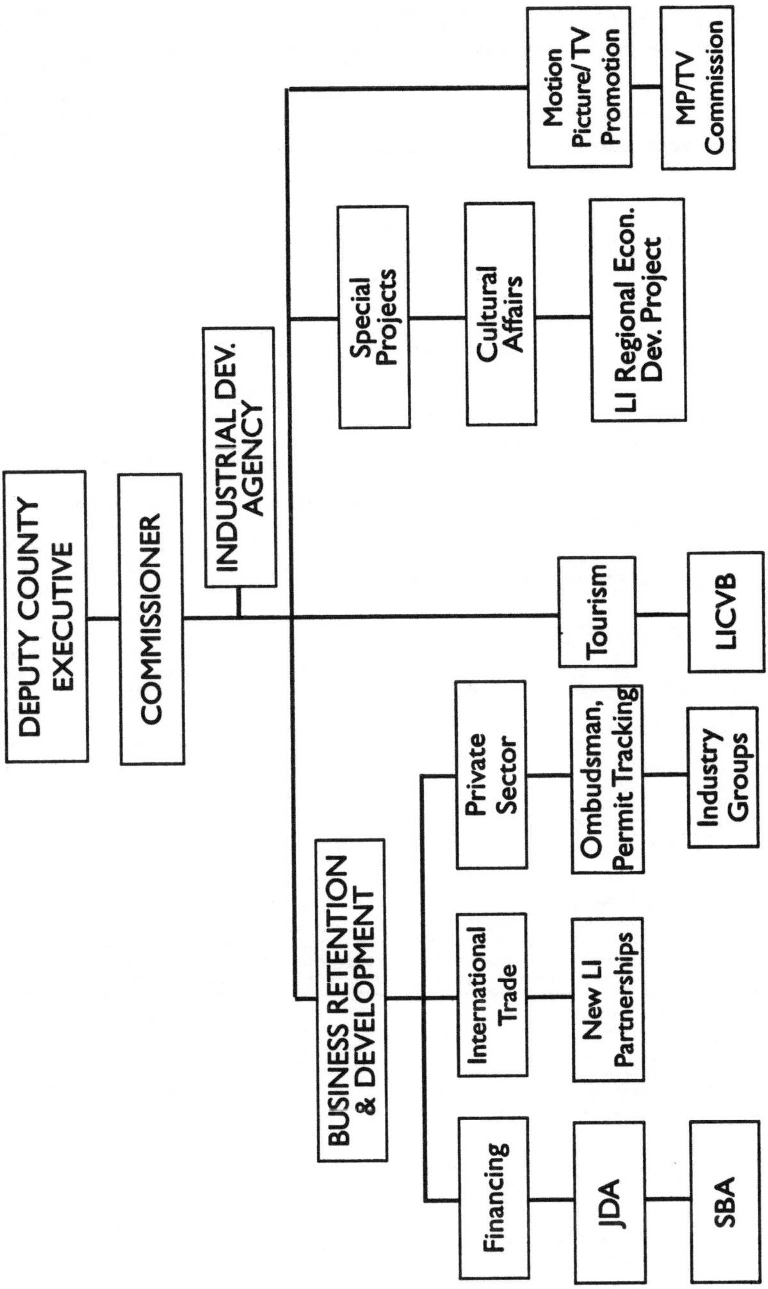

SUFFOLK COUNTY DEPARTMENT OF

CIVIL SERVICE

Robert J. Gaffney
Suffolk County Executive

ANNOUNCES:

PRESS RELEASE
NOVEMBER 1995-13

PUBLIC NOTICE

This brief is an unofficial summary of upcoming examinations. It is recommended that applicants see official examination announcements for complete details. Copies of the official announcements, applications and Transcript/Requesting Routing Forms (CSX26) are available from the Suffolk County Department of Civil Service in Hauppauge or at the Riverhead County Center. Our address in Hauppauge is 220 Rabro Drive, P.O. Box 6100, Hauppauge NY 11788-0099.

TELEPHONE NUMBERS

Suffolk County Department of Civil Service Information Unit 853-5500. Our FAX number is 853-4796.

NEW APPLICATION FORMS

Computer scannable application forms must be used for all examinations given after September 1, 1994.

Open-competitive examinations will require two forms:
- CS-205A (current white application)
- CS-205B (scannable form)

Promotional examinations will require one form:
- CS-203 (scannable form)

APPLICATION PROCESSING FEE

A separate application is required for each examination (identified by examination number) for which you are applying. Each application MUST be accompanied by a non-refundable, non-transferable application processing fee. Unless otherwise noted on the examination announcement, the application processing fee is $15.00 for each application filed. DO NOT SEND CASH. Make your check or money order payable to the Suffolk County Department of Civil Service. Please indicate the examination title and your social security number on the face of your check or money order.

OPEN FILING SYSTEM

The Suffolk county Department of Civil Service accepts applications for most titles before a test is announced.

CONTINUOUS RECRUITMENT

We have several examinations which are being offered on a continuous recruitment basis. For more information please call (516) 853-5500.

APPLICATIONS FOR EXAMINATIONS THAT INVOLVE TRAINING AND EXPERIENCE EVALUATIONS

A candidate who filed for a training and experience examination more than six months prior to the last filing date is advised to amend his or her application to include current information. Candidates are also advised to request from the Department of Civil Service a copy of the official examination announcement which fully describes all the information that must be included in your application. (When critical information is vague or missing, candidates may receive no credit for that part.)

LAST FILING DATE: DECEMBER 6, 1995 **WRITTEN TEST DATE: JANUARY 6, 1996**

SPECIFICATION #	TITLE	BI-WEEKLY SALARY
0251	BUDGET ANALYST PR	$1149 Grade 19
0241	BUDGET EXAMINER OC	$1199 Grade 20
1224	CHIEF ENVIRONMENTAL ANALYST OC	Usual Bi-Weekly Salary $1725-$1999**
7173	COMMUNICATION S TECHNICIAN I OC	$1383 Grade 20 Step 1

The Planning Department

In recent years, this County department has been receiving more attention by the general population. As communities grow and land resources become more intensely used, government officials receive more letters from citizens and more questions at County legislative meetings.

Young citizens need to be made aware that they live in a world that now has close to five billion human beings each needing food, clothing, water, housing, and general living space. Crowded conditions create many problems and our youth need to be challenged to be ready to help solve these problems.

The study of the role of the planning department creates an opportunity to discuss how the student can begin to think of ways to solve the problems being faced today by citizens living in their community. Youngsters respond very positively when made aware of a problem and being asked to solve it. A look at what responsibilities the planning department carries out follows.

1. It collects and analyzes land use and environmental data to prepare management recommendations pertaining to bays, watersheds, fragile shorelines, and associated natural habitats. This includes preserving the quality of groundwater recharge, and maintaining the water quality of surface waters to assure that bathing beaches are not closed to swimming.

2. It advises the County executive and legislature about the purchase of certain land or coastal tracts so that

private housing can't be built on this environmentally fragile land (The Pine Barrens is a good example).

3. It conducts land use studies to determine where shopping centers should be located, where roads should be built, and recommends the size of a building plot of land in housing development (one acre, half-acre, etc.).

4. The planning department researches the effects of hurricanes and coastal storms on the seashore and reports the findings to the County executive and legislature for them to take proper protective action on behalf of the citizens living in those threatened areas of the County.

5. The effects of water pollution on clamming beds are studied. Water pollution effects the economy by preventing clammers from earning a living and also creates a shortage of clams in the marketplace. This deprives people who enjoy eating clams and also increases the price because of the law of supply and demand.

6. It updates County maps as new road and streets are created. Many people depend on updated maps to conduct their daily work (postal workers, UPS, salespersons, real estate agents, etc.). Map-makers are called cartographers.

7. It recommends enactment of new laws that will help to improve the environment and to regulate industries that may be polluting the environment.

DEPARTMENT: PLANNING

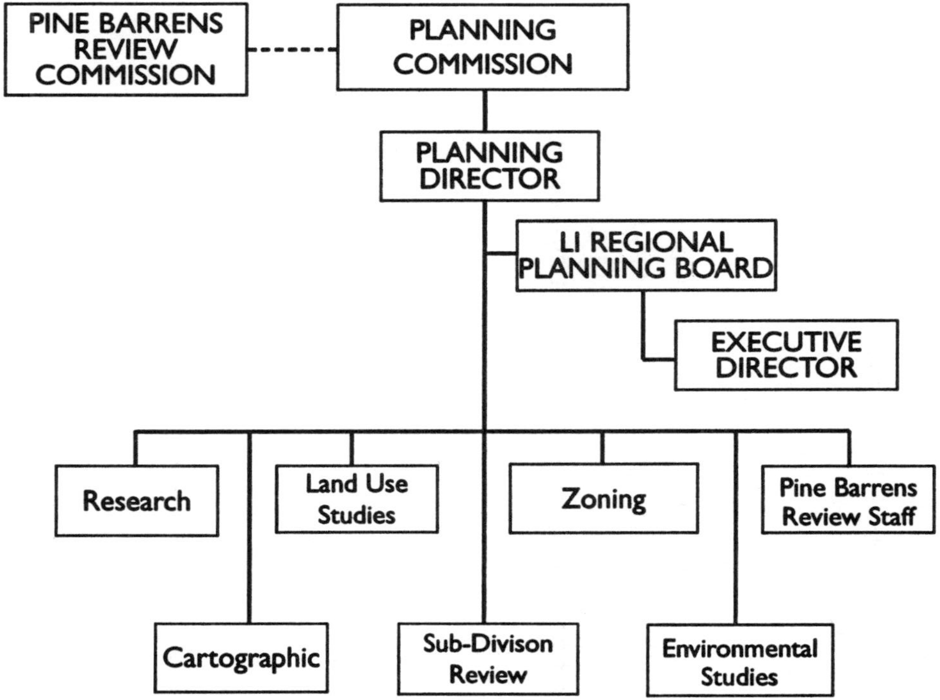

The Legal Aid Society Department

This department is charged with the responsibility of providing legal assistance to citizens charged with a criminal act or family court matters and who are unable to able to pay for a lawyer to defend them. The department is administered by a board of directors appointed by the County executive and approved by the County legislature. Attorneys interested in working in this department are interviewed for the position. Staff members are paid a salary.

An attorney working in this department would make an excellent guest speaker. Teachers should prepare questions that would be asked by students during the guest speaker's visit to the class. A suggested list follows.

DEPARTMENT: LEGAL AID SOCIETY

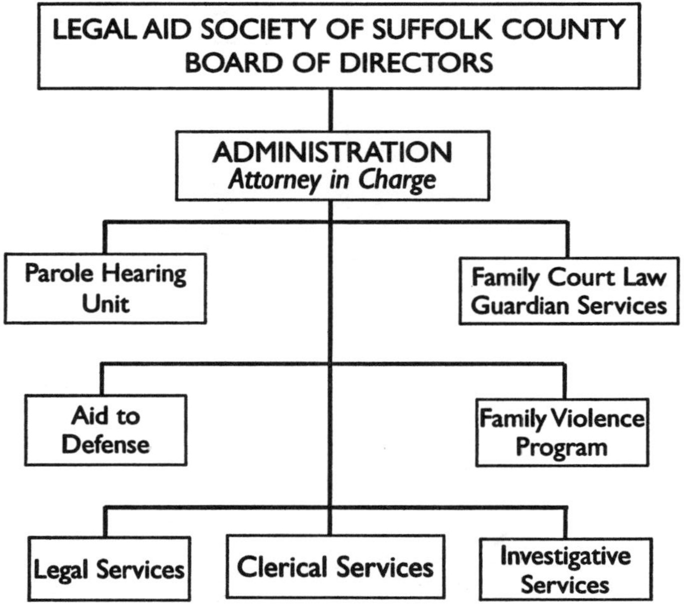

SUGGESTED QUESTIONS TO ASK AN ATTORNEY OF THE LEGAL AID SOCIETY DEPARTMENT

1. What kind of cases have you handled?

2. What made you decide to work in the legal aid department?

3. What kinds of questions were you asked when you were interviewed for the position?

4. What made you decide to become an attorney?

5. How much money can you earn as a staff member of the legal aid society?

6. How do you go about interviewing your client?

7. Can you refuse to handle a case?

8. How are cases assigned to the staff members?

9. What kind of training is necessary for a person to become an attorney (lawyer)?

10. What advice could you give us to become more politically astute?

Students should develop a heightened appreciation of our justice system and the essential role of this department—to assure that a person accused of a crime receives adequate assistance for his/her defense and thus a fair trial.

The Probation Department

This department is responsible for doing investigations and providing services for the County court system. Students need to understand that when convicted criminals receive a jail sentence, serve their time, and are put on probation, they need to be under strict supervision.

In our County, there are many ex-convicts who complete their debt to society on probation. Those on probation need to follow certain rules, find a job, be restricted to a specific location, report periodically to the probation officer, and follow a curfew (time-limit) as to when (s)he can be out of his/her home. Probation officers spend much time in the field. They make home visits and visit the place of work of the person on probation to see how (s)he is doing on the job. The duties carried out by the probation department are seven-fold:

1. It furnishes character profiles on people to the courts before sentencing.

2. It provides background data on detainees (persons being held for sentencing) to help the courts in deciding eligibility for legal aid services.

3. The family circumstances of families seeking to adopt a child are investigated.

4. It supervises persons serving probation time.

5. When necessary, it counsels those on probation as to where to find a job or receive job-training details.

6. It administers group homes for juveniles who committed a non-serious crime and need to be rehabilitated in a minimum security detention facility.

7. Lastly, the probation department helps resolve family conflicts that could lead to serious repercussions.

A director, appointed by the County executive and approved by the County legislature, administers the department. Most staff members are civil service employees and are represented by the municipal employees union.

Thousands of youthful offenders are handled by this department. A talk by a guest speaker from this department would be very enlightening (if not sobering!) to students. It would certainly provide a deterrent for those susceptible to the sort of inappropriate behavior that could bring them before the court system. Teachers should prepare questions for use by students during visit of guest speaker. Suggested questions to ask guest speaker follow.

DEPARTMENT: PROBATION

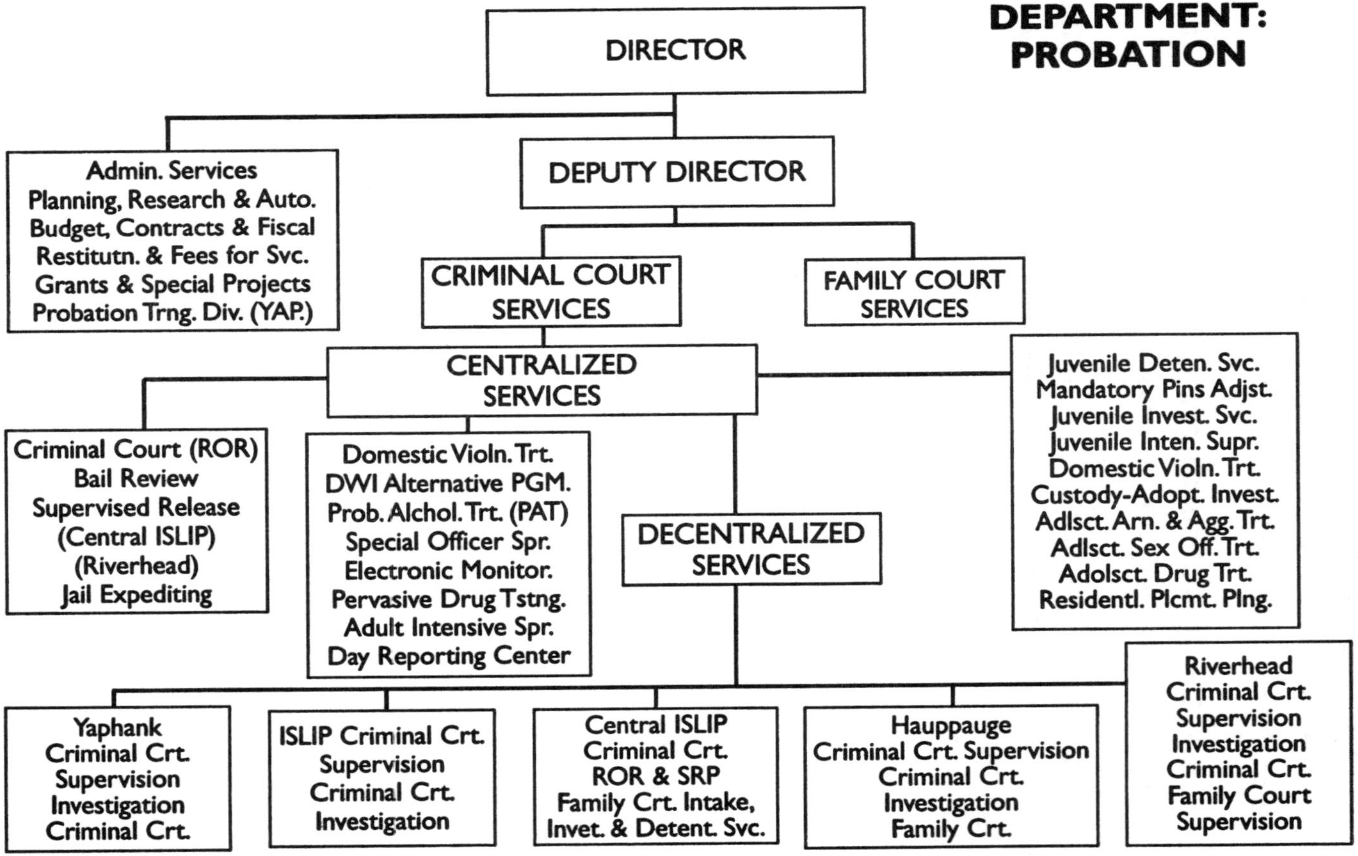

SUGGESTED QUESTIONS FOR THE PROBATION OFFICER

1. How did you get your position?

2. What made you decide to be a probation officer?

3. What are the necessary requirements for the position?

4. How much education is necessary to do the job well?

5. Would you recommend the position to us? Why?

6. What interesting experiences have you had?

7. How much do you earn?

8. How are cases assigned to probation officers?

9. What kinds of questions were you asked when you were interviewed for the position?

10. Are there ample opportunities for advancement in your field of work?

11. What would be your advice as to how young citizens can become more politically astute?

The Soil and Water Conservation Department

Fertile soil and adequate water supplies play a vital part in our daily life. People generally take it for granted that there is plenty of water and that there is a more than adequate supply of fertile soil.

An ongoing education of land utilization is carried out by federal, state, and County government departments to help farmers raise healthy food. Soil can become unproductive, or produce poor-quality food, if it is used overly much without being properly replenished with the fertilizers and minerals that plants need to grow to maturity.

This department was created to develop, recommend, and achieve conservation measures for preserving soil and water resources. Study of this department will prove to be refreshing to the students as they come to realize that water and fertile soil are in short supply throughout the world, and need to be preserved. The soil and water conservation department carries out the following responsibilities:

1. It tries to control floods that will wash away top soil.

2. It helps farmers provide proper drainage of excess waters from heavy rainfalls.

3. It assists farmers to prevent soil erosion by use of crop-rotation. Certain grown plants take nutrients away from the soil, while certain plants add nutrients.

4. It conducts research on ways to produce greater crop yields on smaller plots of land.

DEPARTMENT: SOIL & WATER CONSERVATION DISTRICT

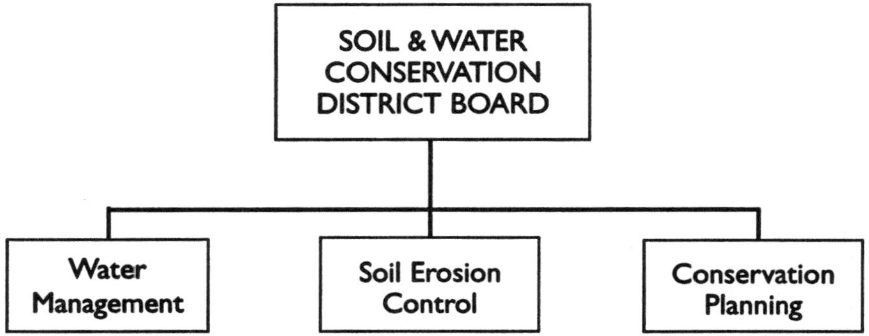

5. It conducts research on how to raise more fertile seeds that will produce better farm products.

6. It helps farmers to lay out irrigation systems to water the crops properly and save them when there are periods of drought.

7. Consultation and technical assistance are provided for land use, soil analysis, water management, and sediment and erosion control.

8. In conclusion, the soil and water department provides information to farmers about use of pesticides to deal with insects that cause crop damage.

This department is governed by a board of directors who are appointed by County legislature. Persons selected to this department need to have background in farming.

The Cooperative Extension Department

This department is charged with the responsibility of providing educational programs for school-age children and the public in the following areas:

1. **Agriculture**

   a. It offers research based information on growing plants.

   b. It presents demonstrations and educational programs that address the needs of a variety of county residents.

DEPARTMENT: COOPERATIVE EXTENSION

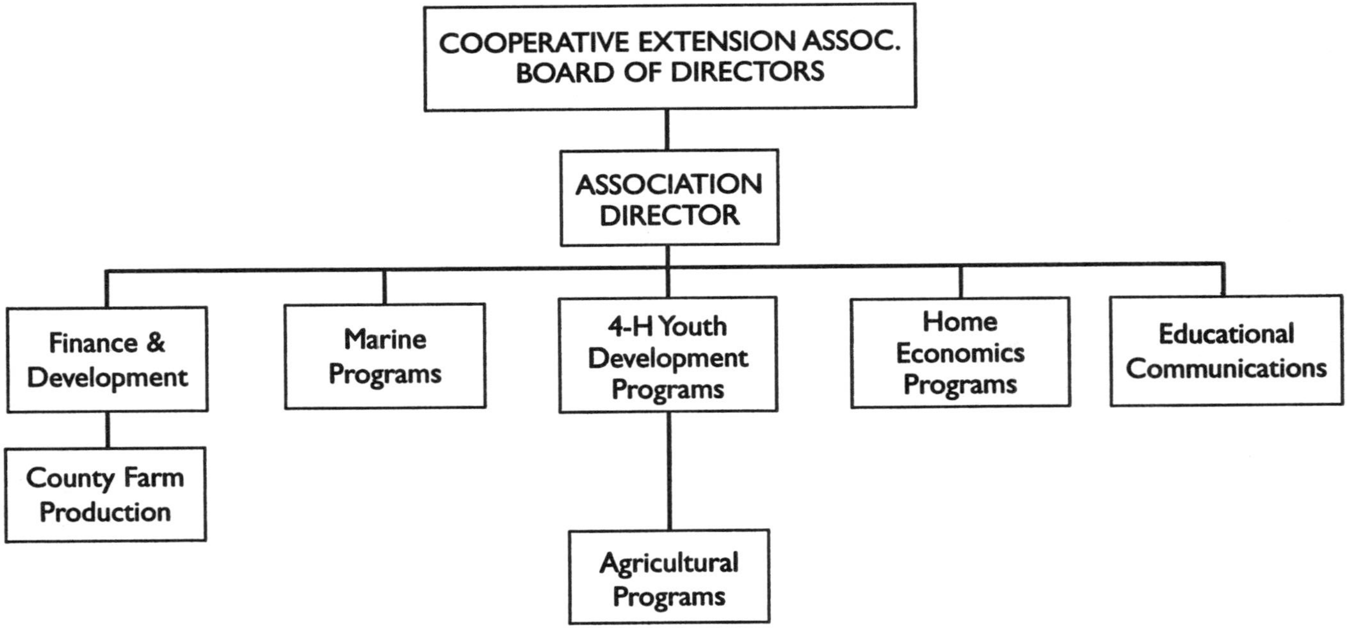

c. It keeps local food growers updated on the latest data relating to labor supply, pest control, and importance of proper use of farm equipment.

d. It operates a horticultural diagnostic lab to help county residents raise healthy plants for house and commercial use.

e. It furnishes trained staff to answer questions about farming from county residents.

2. **Home Economics**

a. It provides educational programs for homemakers to prepare healthy meals.

b. It provides educational programs for county residents to be able to purchase more food at less cost and greater nutritional value.

3. **4-H Youth Development**
(HEAD-HAND-HEART-HEALTH)

a. It provides educational programs and materials for youths, five to 19 years old, interested in learning about farming and eating healthy foods.

b. It organizes 4-H clubs to train youth to live healthy lives by eating the right kind of foods and to practice good health habits that will increase life span and enjoyment of life. 4-H members learn about animals and how to take care of them. Competition is encouraged to grow the best plant and raise the healthiest animal. Prizes are awarded during annual exhibitions held by 4-H leaders.

d. Schools are visited to recruit 4-H members and explain member benefits.

4. **County Farm and Education Center**

a. It encourages field trips by school groups to visit County farms and learn about animal husbandry (breeding) and land cultivation.

b. It holds periodic special events and festivals and invites the public to attend. Trained personnel conduct tours and answer questions about farming.

5. **Marine Program**

a. It assists coastal residents to better use their valuable marine resources.

b. It conducts studies of coastline environment, sharing results of these studies with fishers, marine businesses and other citizens interested in improving the environment and protecting the County's economy.

c. It directs a marine environmental learning center. All interested residents are invited to attend lectures given by this center.

6. **County Food Purchases**

a. Food that is raised on the County farm is sold to the sheriff's department and County infirmary for use by prisoners and patients.

b. Profits from the food raised helps to lower the cost of running this important department.

The cooperative extension department is managed by a board of directors appointed by the County legislature. An association director manages the day to day operations of the department.

The Fire, Rescue, and Emergency Services Department

When unexpected disastrous events take place, this department must be ready to provide emergency assistance at a moment's notice. Hurricanes, forest fires, earthquakes, floods, and accidents that cause large scale damage must be responded to by this department. They coordinate local fire and rescue units so that a minimum loss of lives and property can be attained. A high-tech communication system is coordinated and maintained with local radio and TV stations to inform the public as to how to react to disastrous events.

They are responsible for training local fire and rescue personnel to respond efficiently to disastrous occurrences. Many trained volunteers are used effectively by this department and past record show they have done an excellent job to protect the lives of county citizens. It can be dangerous work. We must constantly recruit volunteers to help this department with their urgent vocation.

It is a department we would like to never use, but records show they have been put to good use countless times in the past. Students should consider volunteering as fire or rescue persons when they reach the proper age.

The fire, rescue, and emergency services department is administered by an APPOINTED commissioner. Ten disciplines are performed by this life-saving crew.

1. A fire academy trains fire personnel. Training includes fighting house fires, fires in industrial buildings, and fires that contain stored toxic chemicals and highly explosive natural gas and gasoline.

2. They train and certify rescue personnel. Emergency medical training is the major part of their education.

3. Emergency shelters are maintained to house persons left homeless due to disasters.

4. They coordinate with public schools and other public institutions to set up plans to provide shelter and food for people affected by disaster such as a hurricane. They train fire marshals to make investigations of home and businesses suspected of violating fire codes and endangering occupants of that kind of buildings.

5. They carry out an extensive program of educating the public on how to react to disasters.

6. They coordinate the efforts of the auxiliary police (volunteer police) to respond to disasters in an effective manner. They conduct training programs for the auxiliary police officers.

DEPARTMENT: FIRE, RESCUE & EMERGENCY SERVICES

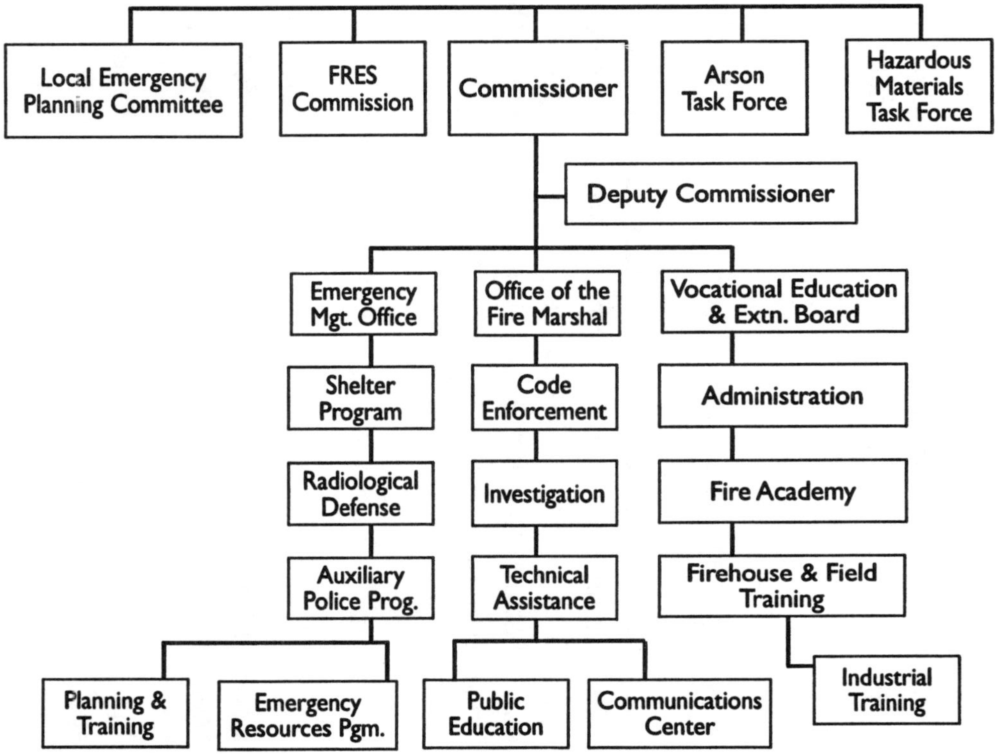

7. They maintain a central communications center, where highly trained personnel are ready to respond to unexpected disaster that takes place.

8. They provide qualified personnel to deal with hazardous materials that need special handling.

9. They conduct periodic emergency drills to re-enact a possible disaster and evaluates how the mock drill was responded to by all involved units.

10. They investigate suspicious fires to determine if they were caused by arson (deliberately started by someone).

A guest appearance by a fire marshal would be an excellent experience for students to have during the study of this department. Teachers could help students prepare pertinent questions to ask the guest speaker and make the experience more meaningful for the students.

The County Legislature

County legislatures, as we know them today, have not existed a long period of time. County government was governed by a BOARD OF SUPERVISORS. Town supervisors met monthly, discussed, and dealt with County matters. This continued until County populations began to grow rapidly. A greater demand for more and better services from the existing County departments motivated concerned citizens to take necessary action.

A supreme court decision ordered the establishment of a County legislature, instead of a board of supervisors, to

DEPARTMENT: LEGISLATURE

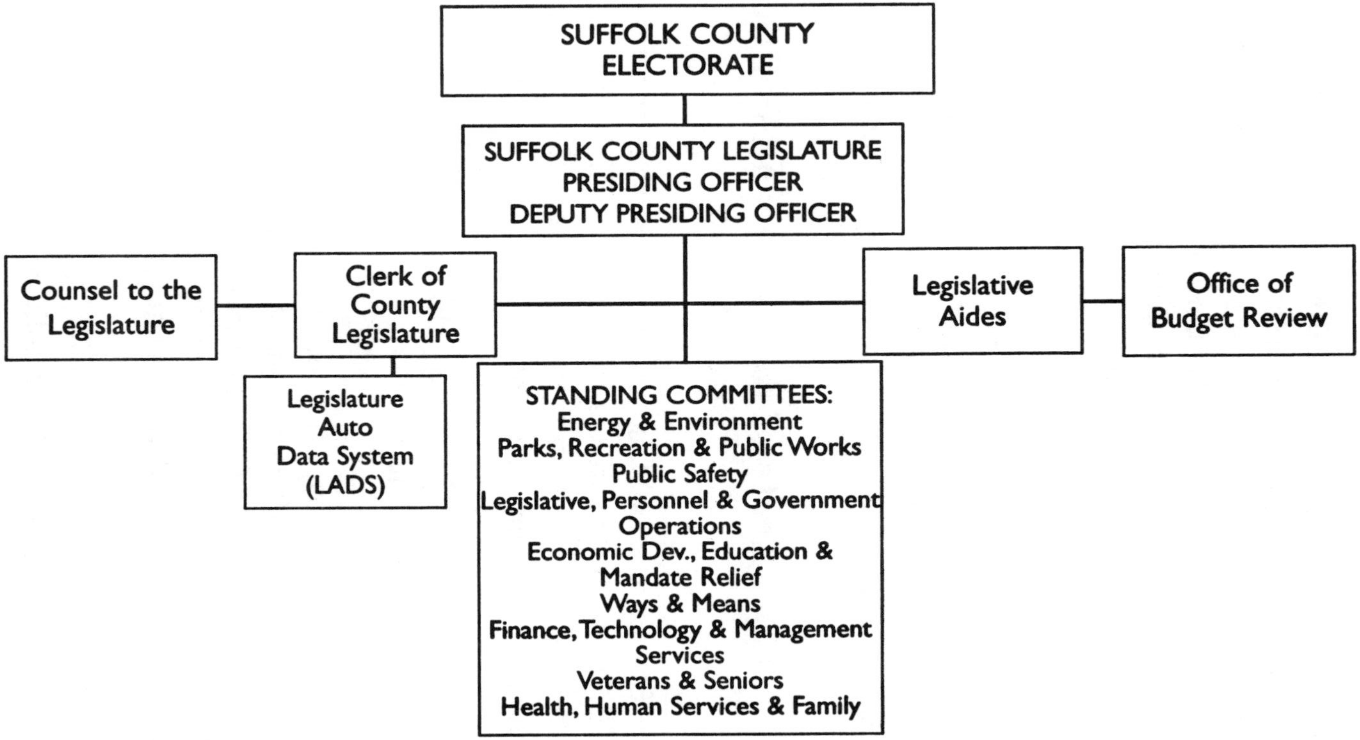

take effect and to ELECT County legislators on a population basis. The County was divided into equally populated legislative districts. Please recall that the smallest unit of political government is the election district. Each election district contains up to 1000 registered voters. The total number of election districts were divided into the number of legislators in the County legislature.

The important point to understand is that County legislators represent a certain number of election districts that contain a certain number of voters. Suffolk County for example, contains 18 legislators, while another County may have 15 or 21, etc., depending on the size and population of the County.

The Effects of the Census on Political Boundaries

Students should be made aware that the taking of a CENSUS, which takes place every TEN years, usually effects the population figures of a legislative district. When the census is completed by the federal government, the census figures are reviewed by the County legislature to determine if the geographic and political divisions of the districts need to be re-districted.

The 1990 census figures showed significant changes in population of Suffolk County and resulted in many citizens having a different County legislator. It also meant that the INCUMBENT legislator (currently in office) had to campaign for votes in districts that (s)he had not represented.

The board of elections has political maps available of legislative districts. These political maps can be used by the teacher to show how populations can change in ten years, leading into a discussion as to how population changes can take place, effecting elections.

Many deliberations take place during re-districting periods, as each of the two major political parties try to draw geographic boundaries that will benefit their own party. This results in more bargaining and arguing between party leaders and interested citizens. Public hearings are held and citizens are given the opportunity to speak on the issues. The next census will take place in the year 2000!

Organization of the County Legislature

The County legislature is responsible for proposing, discussing, and enacting County laws. It is also responsible for checking to ensure that the laws they pass are being carried out by the County executive and his many departments. Since laws are not always properly enforced by the executive branch of government, the legislature must keep a vigilant eye on how the County government is operating on behalf of the citizens. A County legislator must keep in close contact with as many of his/her constituents as is humanly possible. Each legislator is permitted to have some staff called legislative aides. (S)he also has a district office to meet constituents and to hold press conferences. Office staff includes a secretary and an office clerk.

The legislator sends periodic newsletters to his electors to keep them both informed of what is happening in County government and what (s)he is doing in the legislature on their behalf. (S)he receives many letters and responds to them as quickly as possible. The average number of voters that a legislator represents is around 40,000. (S)he is usually invited to make speaking engagements on a regular basis. These engagements usually help express his/her philosophy of government. The legislator gleans how his/her constituency feels about how well (s)he is representing them in County government.

Elections are held every TWO years. Some citizens have been suggesting the term of the County legislator be extended to four years. Their argument is that if (s)he has to run for election every two years, the legislator has to constantly campaign for office, and doesn't have the proper time to do the job effectively.

The County legislature follows a scheduled calendar of events. The times and places of all meetings are published in advance so that interested citizens can make plans to attend them. The County legislature usually meets twice a month. Some meetings are held in the evening hours, some in the daytime hours.

On the first business day of each calendar year, an ORGANIZATIONAL MEETING is held, wherein the PRESIDING OFFICER and the DEPUTY PRESIDING OFFICER are ELECTED by the County legislators by a majority vote.

The legislative responsibilities of the **presiding officer** are five-fold:

1. Chairing the legislative meetings.
2. Calling special meetings of the legislature when (s)he deems necessary.

3. Assigning each resolution (bill) to a standing or special committee for its review.

4. Setting up the various committees of the legislature.

5. Appointing legislators to the various committees and the chairperson of each committee.

The presiding officer is given extra staff to handle his/her responsibilities and earns a higher salary. Salaries for County legislators range from $35,000 to $50,000 per year.

The deputy presiding officer runs meetings and other legislative responsibilities in the absence of the presiding officer. (S)he also has extra staff to help him/her to carry out the duties of that position. (S)he also is paid a higher salary than the other County legislators.

Standing Committees

Students should become aware that MOST of the business conducted by County legislators is done in standing committees. Each committee is assigned a particular area of County government and at these meetings discusses a proposed resolution that relates to that area of government.

An example is the energy and environment committee. This committee is concerned with matters that deal with our sources of energy and the state of our environment and any resolutions being proposed to deal with this area are considered by this committee.

There are nine standing committees in County legislatures. They include:

1. Energy and environment

2. Parks, recreation, and public works

3. Public safety

4. Legislative, personnel, and government operations

5. Economic development, education and mandate relief

6. Ways and means

7. Finance, technology and management services

8. Veterans and seniors

9. Health, human services, and family

Each of these committees has a chairperson, appointed by the presiding officer and several legislators selected from the major parties in the legislature (Democratic, Republican). These committees meet regularly and hold public meetings so that citizens can attend and contribute their thoughts on pending resolutions. These meetings are not always well attended but make excellent opportunities for students to meet County legislators on a more informal basis and ask questions about their role in government. The author has had many field trips of this kind to standing committee meetings and has found legislators amenable to interacting with students in attendance.

A field trip to one of these meetings helps the teacher to reinforce the work done in the class about the County legislature. The "hands-on" experiences make the study of government more relevant to the students, motivating them to want more of these kind of experiences.

Standing committees vote after discussing the pros and cons of each proposed resolution. If the MAJORITY vote in favor of the resolution, it is then sent to the FULL LEGISLATURE for further discussion, including the holding of a public hearing to enable citizens to speak on the proposed resolution. This takes time.

Students will learn that passing laws is not a simple procedure. Some resolutions get TABLED (put on hold for a future meeting). Meanwhile, other resolutions receive the attention of the legislature. Delays may cause the proposed resolution to lose support from the legislators who initially supported it. Thus, some proposed resolutions "die" in committee, some get tabled, some lose by a vote of the legislature, and others are passed by a majority vote. Most proposed resolutions never get to become County laws. The same holds true in the state assembly, state senate, and U.S. Congress.

Once a proposed resolution is passed by the County legislature, it is sent to the County executive for his/her signature to make it become an official County law (resolution). If (s)he is against the proposed resolution, (s)he has the right to VETO the proposed resolution. The veto means that (s)he is against the resolution and does not want to see it become a law.

The vetoed resolution is then returned to the County legislature. At that time, it takes another vote on the proposed resolution. If the legislature OVERRIDES the veto by a two-thirds majority, the resolution automatically becomes a law and the County executive has to enforce that resolution. An override of a veto does not happen very often. It is not easy to have two thirds of the legislature vote to override the County executive's veto.

While the proposing, discussing and passing laws is a major part of the responsibility of the legislature, it is also important for them to make sure that the resolutions (laws) are being carried out and enforced by the executive department. This is called LEGISLATIVE OVERSIGHT. The County legislature is the watchdog for citizens in County government.

The County Legislative Meeting

The scheduled meeting of the full body of legislatures is an interesting event. An AGENDA (a list of things that need to be dealt with) is published and distributed to the citizens in attendance. The meeting is called to order by the presiding officer and a roll call is taken by the clerk of the legislature. Each legislator states that he is present for the meeting. The pledge of allegiance is taken at all public meetings. Sometimes a moment of silence is called for by the presiding officer to commemorate the death of a notable citizen or political figure.

During the meeting each item on the agenda is taken in the order listed. These meetings can sometimes go on for a long period of time depending on the nature of the contents of the agenda. Some items are very controversial and result in much heated debate. All the proceedings of the meeting are recorded by the clerk of the legislature.

As the meeting goes on, legislative aides pop in and out of the meeting to bring some needed papers that the legislator asked for. Sometimes legislators talk with one another while someone else is at the microphone speaking. They appear to be rude, but this kind of conversation takes place between legislators to get some question answered that directly relates to the meeting going on. Legislators have to be good listeners and must be able to think quickly in order to participate effectively at these legislative meetings. They must be able to absorb a lot of information and be well-informed on many issues.

All legislative meetings are attended by television crews who do interviews of citizens that are going to make a presentation to the legislature, interview legislators or an invited County department administrator who will make a report to the legislature during that meeting. Newspaper reporters are also in attendance so they can record the highlights of the meeting and write an article that will appear in the newspaper the next day.

Some meetings get heated over controversial issues such as the resolution on "no smoking" in restaurants. Many citizens from both sides of the issue attended this meeting and there were strong speeches made. Some of the meetings can appear to be dull and uninteresting. This is part of the price we pay, living in a democracy. There is no rush to make quick decisions. In the long run this results in fewer laws that need to be enforced, instead of having too many laws and much difficulty enforcing them.

The Annual County Budget

Each year, a County budget must be prepared by the County executive and sent to the County legislature for approval and passage. This is a very important, but time-consuming process. The office of legislative budget review—a particular office in the County legislature—studies the County budget. This office also provides analytical and oversight services for the County legislature.

The **Director of Budget Review** and his professional staff are responsible for:

1. Determining the extent to which legislative policies are being competently enforced by the executive officials.

2. Determining whether County programs are achieving their legal objectives.

3. Reviewing the performance and management of County department heads and other County agencies.

4. Analyzing the soundness of departmental budget estimates and monetary requests throughout the year.

5. Analyzing the proposed capital (purchase of expensive items) budget. This could include purchase of vehicles, road building equipment, County buildings, property, etc.

6. Reviewing the County operating budget (costs of all other items needed to run the County). An example would be salaries of all county workers, paper, gasoline to run all county vehicles, etc.

7. Determining whether the County has adequate plans, organizations, facilities, and controls for the optimal (best) accomplishments for all legislative policies and programs.

The budget review office submits written reports and makes recommendations for change to the legislature. This office also provides information on the fiscal impact (effect) of proposed legislation. It provides the legislature several legislator reference manuals, a book on County board and commissions and a source book on all County revenues.

Clerk of the County Legislature

This APPOINTED person has an important role in the County Legislature. (S)he is responsible for taking care of the following:

1. Maintaining records of all legislative proceedings.

2. Routing all resolutions passed by the legislature to the proper County departments.

3. Keeping records of all local laws passed and made available to interested persons.

4. Maintaining records assigned to this department.

A chief deputy clerk and a deputy clerk assist the clerk of the County legislature to carry out his/her responsibilities. An office staff is also available to the clerk and his/her deputies.

Counsel to the County Legislature

This selected person provides the legal advice that legislators need to write resolutions that are not confusing nor conflict with resolutions already existing. The counsel attends the regularly scheduled full legislature meetings and is periodically asked questions by legislators in attendance about legal matters that need clarification (explaining) or interpretation (making clear). It is a responsible position and this person must be very learned about municipal and County laws. (S)he is provided a staff of law clerks who do necessary research.

(S)he may also be invited to attend standing committee meetings to help clarify a proposed resolution. Before a local law (resolution) may be introduced by any legislator, it must be presented to the counsel to the legislature who must then deliver a memorandum to the clerk of the legislature, as to form, legal significance, and possible budgetary impact of the proposed local law (resolution).

Special Committee

The presiding officer may appoint a special committee whenever necessary. They are also called *AD HOC* committees since they serve for a particular purpose and are terminated when they complete it.

Memorializing

Occasionally, the county may wish to officially state its position on legislation or actions pending in another legislative body. This can be done by a memorializing resolution. The procedure for a memorializing resolution is not the same as for a regular resolution.

Legislators are elected for a term of two years. Some County legislators have voted to limit the number of years that a County legislator can serve. Twelve years is the average limit that most legislatures have voted into law.

A field trip to a County legislative meeting would be an absorbing experience for students that the teacher can use to practically instruct them about the County legislature on how it is organized and operates.

QUESTIONS TO ASK A COUNTY LEGISLATOR GUEST SPEAKER

1. How long have you been serving in the County legislature?

2. How do you go about running for County Legislator?

3. How did you decide to become a member of your political party instead of another party?

4. What are your priorities as you try to represent the people from your legislative district?

5. What do you see as the critical issues that face the people of our County?

6. What would you suggest to try to encourage young students to become more politically astute?

7. Do you intend to run for higher office in the future? When will you know when to consider running for a higher office?

8. When did you yourself decide to run for public office?

9. What person, if any, played an important role in helping you to decide to become politically involved?

10. What should young citizens do to become effectively involved in the political process?

11. Why do you think young citizens are not more actively involved politically?

12. What role should our schools play in helping our young citizens to become politically astute?

13. What committees do you serve on? How were you selected?

14. What role does the counsel to the legislature play? How do you utilize his/her services?

15. What is your opinion on how the presiding officer is doing his/her job?

16. Do you work with the office of legislative budget review?

17. Do you think the County legislature is doing enough legislative oversight on the County departments?

Introduction to Political Parties

What is a political party? A political party is an organization formed by citizens who have a similar political PHILOSOPHY. A party is concerned with: how government should serve its citizens; how we should relate to other nations, how we should help others in need; how we should educate our children; how big or how small our government should be; how big or how small our armed forces should be; how we should deal with moral issues such as pro-life or pro-choice. These ISSUES contribute to the formation of political parties.

As citizens listen to candidates explain the philosophy of the political party they represent, they make the important decision of whether they agree or disagree with the candidate speaking. After listening to the candidates that represent different political views on the issues, the citizen can make several decisions:

1. (S)he can decide to vote for that party candidate.

2. (S)he can decide to make a financial contribution to help that candidate get his/her philosophy to other citizens.

3. (S)he can decide to actively participate in the political campaign and help that person get elected.

4. (S)he can decide to become an active member of that political party and participate in helping other candidates to also get elected.

5. (S)he can decide to learn more about the organization of that political party and prepare to run for office to represent that political party.

6. (S)he can become a member of the staff of the candidate (S)he helped to get elected once the candidate takes office as an elected official.

These are the options offered to ALL citizens that want to participate in the POLITICAL PROCESS. If a citizen decides to remain "in the back seat" and not participate, the chances are that people with selfish motives will seek these offices and serve not the public but themselves, and their selfishly motivated supporters.

What is a philosophy? The Webster's Dictionary defines philosophy to mean the following: "a system of principles (rules) for guidance in practical affairs of every day life." The word derives from the Greek words *philos* (meaning "love of") and *sophus* ("wisdom"). A basic definition of a philosopher could be someone who loves wisdom and wants to live in harmony with others and share that love and wisdom with others.

Thus a political philosophy basically means the combined caring of a group of people with a similar desire to promote the general welfare of the community (nation, state, county, village) for the good of all the citizens living there. Basically all political parties desire to serve the needs of the people living in the COMMUNITY. The DIFFERENCE results in HOW the different political parties want to go about doing just that.

Political Factions

What is a political faction? The Webster's Dictionary defines faction as "a group or clique within a larger group, party, government organization." As a young citizen just starting to learn to become politically astute, it is important for you to understand this term and how it applies to political parties.

Now that we know what political parties are, we need to explore political factions. We need to now introduce three political terms that you will be hearing whenever discussions on politics and candidates take place. These three terms are:

1. LIBERAL

2. MODERATE

3. CONSERVATIVE

Within each political party are members who consider themselves one of the three terms just listed. People like to categorize or label candidates and the MEDIA (newspapers, radio, TV, etc.) use these labels to help identify the factions in each party. As a young citizen you have the right to ask, at this point, why these differences? That is a very good question that is not easy to define.

What is known about human nature is that whenever any issue is discussed, people take different positions on that issue. Some are STRONGLY for the ISSUE, some are STRONGLY against the issue, and others are not sure of whether they are for or against that issue. Thus there are THREE positions related to that one issue. For example, some people are very PRO-LIFE, some are very PRO-CHOICE, and some are not sure how they stand or take an "it doesn't matter attitude." Thus there are three sides to that single, important issue.

Within EACH political wing you will find each of these FACTIONS existing side by side taking various positions on the issues being discussed. A working definition of "liberal" could be the following: a person who wants to make changes in the existing way of life. A "liberal" could also be defined as someone who is anxious for quick change. A "moderate" could be someone who knows that changes are necessary but doesn't want to move too quickly with these changes. A "conservative" could be someone who does not want to see any changes and wants to keep the status quo.

These three main factions struggle for the control of the party leadership and thus much discussion and give and take place during the selection of candidates that will represent that party. Young citizens need to know that living in a democracy can be exciting once you know how the system works and how to become ACTIVELY INVOLVED. Usually the faction that dominates major parties is the MODERATE faction. Another term used for faction is WING of the party.

The County Political Chairperson

As was mentioned in our study of town government, each town has a political leader who carries a great deal of political power. In the County political structure, there is another political leader called the County chairman of each political party. This person is ELECTED by the members of the County party committee. You will recall that the members of the committee were also ELECTED by the voters in each ELECTION DISTRICT.

Students should be taught that the committee persons ELECTED by voters of the election district that are REGISTERED in a particular party (Republican, Democratic) These elections are held in September of ODD years and are called PRIMARY ELECTIONS.

When the election is over, each committee person receives from the board of elections a CERTIFICATE OF ELECTION TO PARTY POSITION, indicating that the person named was ELECTED to the position of MEMBER OF COUNTY COMMITTEE.

In this capacity, the committee person has the responsibility of electing the town leader AND the County leader of his party. Many members of the town political committee and the County political committee are APPOINTED by the COUNTY CHAIRPERSON with the approval of the town chairperson.

Too often, there is a lack of interest in the election district for anyone to run for that position. The position has no salary and a person must have a desire to participate in the political process by giving of his/her time to the voters in his/her district and help select viable candidates that will represent the community effectively. Review of the town political leader will make students become more knowledgeable about the responsibilities and authority of the County political leader.

Certificate of Election to Party Position

BOARD OF ELECTIONS
SUFFOLK COUNTY, N.Y.

This is to certify that at the PRIMARY ELECTION held in and for the COUNTY OF SUFFOLK, on the...........day of September, 1982,..was duly elected by the Conservative party to the party position of COUNTY COMMITTEEMAN in and for the....................................Election District of the Town of..

In Witness whereof, we have hereunto set our hands and affixed the seal of the BOARD OF ELECTIONS on this......day of September, 1982.

OFFICIAL SEAL
SUFFOLK
COUNTY
N.Y.
BOARD OF ELECTIONS

Everett F. McNab
Commissioner

Frank Gold
Commissioner
Board of Elections
Yaphank, N.Y.

The County chairperson receives a salary and it is a full time position requiring him/her to work long hours (especially during the evening hours) during political campaign periods.

Understanding Our Judical System

Students, at this level of their intellectual development need to build a solid foundation of our courts. At the village level, the student became acquainted with the village justice who deliberates (tries) minor cases such as traffic tickets, and violation of village laws (building codes, health laws, etc.).

In larger, more populated towns the court system is known as the district court. In smaller, less populated towns, the courts have town justices.

In either case the judges try lawbreakers and interpret the laws. Serious violations of the law called FELONIES can be tried in a district court along with traffic violations and other infractions not conforming to town ordinances (laws).

Thus, a student visiting a district court can see a judge trying a traffic violation, a felony (armed robbery, murder), and a less serious crime called a MISDEMEANOR. The objective to understand is that district court judges and town justices handle cases that fall into the jurisdiction (authority, area) of the town.

The judges are ELECTED for a six year term. Judges CANNOT campaign like other candidates for office. They can speak to groups that invite him/her to speak but (s)he is limited to speaking about the JUDICIAL PROCESS and can not try to convince listeners as to who is the better qualified candidate for judge.

Small Claims Court

One of the interesting divisions of the district court is the small claims court. This court is provided to the citizens of the town to seek REDRESS (correction, repair) of a contract between citizens that conducted a business transaction. Thousands of cases are handled every year by the district court who set aside one day a week to handle these cases.

For example, a person signs an agreement (contract) with another person to repair a roof. The person who is supposed to repair the roof does not do any work it. The person who wanted the roof repaired goes to the district court and gets a legal paper called a subpoena (summons) to order the person who was supposed to do the roof to appear in court before the district court judge at a certain time.

The subpoena is delivered by hand and a paper stating that (s)he received the subpoena is signed. If the person who received the subpoena does not appear in court (s)he is held in CONTEMPT OF COURT and can be arrested and serve a period of time in jail.

On the day of the COURT HEARING, the judge calls the two persons who have the dispute to his/her bench and asks them if they can settle the dispute by discussing the difficulty. If they agree, the judge writes a decision on what they decide and this decision MUST be carried out by the two parties in the dispute. If no agreement can be reached, the two parties present their views and any documents that will prove their case. No lawyer need be present at these hearings. There is no jury for these kinds of cases. The judge renders a verdict in writing and both parties have to follow the terms of the verdict.

A visit to a small claims court session would be most intriguing to the students. Usually the judge will take time during his/her appearance to explain to those in attendance how the small claims court operates. Small claims court handles cases that involve damages or loss of services under $1,000.

NOTE: A small claims guide is available through the district court administrative office.

Here is a list of the types of cases handled in a small claims court:

1. A tenant refuses to pay the rent to the landlord.

2. Someone hits another person's car and causes minor damages but refuses to pay.

3. Someone buys an appliance (refrigerator, washer, etc.) and the dealer delivers a damaged appliance, refusing to replace the appliance.

4. You purchase a ring that is supposed to be diamond and you find it is not a diamond.

5. A mechanic fixes your car. Though it still runs poorly, he refuses to work further on your car.

6. You hire a catering hall for a wedding but you decide to cancel the wedding, and the manager of the catering hall refuses to refund your deposit.

Courtroom Conduct

Sometimes emotions can run high during the hearing because people are angry and start yelling at each other. The court has trained court officers who are there to maintain proper courtroom conduct. The small claims court plays an intricate role in our judicial system, settling disputes between citizens at, or before they reach, "the boiling point."

QUESTIONS TO ASK JUDGE ON FIELD TRIP TO SMALL CLAIMS COURT:

1. What qualifications must a judge have to make good court decisions?

2. When did you decide that you wanted to become a judge?

3. What made you decide that you wanted to become a judge?

4. What person in your life influenced you to make law your career?

5. What advice would you give us if we wanted to become a judge?

6. Why is it important to understand how our legal system operates?

7. What are some interesting cases you have heard?

8. How do you campaign when you try to be elected as a judge?

9. What advice would you give us to become involved in politics?

10. When is the best time to get involved in politics?

11. How do I decide what political party I should join?

The County Surrogate Court

Many citizens throughout our country DO NOT make a WILL (a document that explains what a person wants done with his/her ASSETS—money, property, etc.—when (s)he dies). Because of this unfortunate reality, a SURROGATE COURT was established. Roget's Thesaurus describes the word surrogate as: 1) agent 2) substitute 3) representative 4) deputy 5) replacement 6) alternate 7) delegate 8) in place of 9) power of attorney. The County surrogate court consists of ONE judge who is elected for a term of six years. (S)he is responsible for carrying out the following responsibilities:

1. (S)he administers the law in ALL matters relating to the affairs of descendant's (dead person's) estate.

2. (S)he probates—defined as 1) authenticates 2) supports 3) upholds 4) attests 5) settles 6) removes all doubts 7) certifies 8) backs up 9) proves 10) confirms—the will of a person who has died.

3. (S)he appoints lawyers to help settle an estate of a deceased person who has not left a Will.

4. (S)he acts as a GUARDIAN (defined as: 1) protector 2) manager 3) administrator 4) executor; source?) of a child's interests in a will containing specifics that show that the deceased left part of his/her property and money to the child to be given to the child when they reach a certain age (for example, 18 or older).

5. When members of a dead person's family contest the will, a hearing is conducted to determine how the deceased's estate is to be distributed.

Students need to appreciate the fact that they should consider making up a will at a certain time in their lives in order to prevent the problems that many citizens incur because of a lack of a will. Students should be encouraged to discuss this important factor of life with their parents. A very readable and important pamphlet is available from the office of the surrogate court that explains the importance of making a will.

The surrogate court judge has a support staff in his/her office to assist in carrying out his/her important responsibilities to the people living in the County. The PUBLIC ADMINISTRATOR helps the surrogate judge to manage the supporting staff all of whom have legal backgrounds.

The County Family Court

The family court has been in existence since 1962. The family court is a CIVIL COURT, and not a CRIMINAL COURT. The judges are ELECTED for a term of six years. The family court carries out the following responsibilities:

1. It has original jurisdiction (authority, control) over juvenile (youthful) delinquents (wrongdoers, offenders).

2. It holds court hearings for students who fail to attend school (truants).

3. It holds court hearings to decide who gets custody of children in families having marital problems.

4. It helps married couples get a child (children) through adoption proceedings.

5. It renders (presents) verdicts (decisions) on how much money a father must give to help support the children in cases of separation of mother and father.

6. It issues a court order of protection to prevent one spouse from physically and emotionally endangering the other spouse.

7. It assigns children, unable to live with their natural families, to foster care parents. These foster parents are thoroughly investigated to see that children are placed in adequate homes, in the care of persons with competent parenting skills.

Decisions of the judges are made without any jury trial and are carried out by members of the court such as probation officers and case workers who investigate the family backgrounds and circumstances, and appear as witnesses during court hearings.

This court is involved in thousands of cases every year. family court judges need to have special skills to handle the delicate situations they face each court day.

The Supreme Court

The supreme court is the highest court in the state. This court has UNLIMITED JURISDICTION (area of authority) in CIVIL and CRIMINAL cases. It is often referred to as the "backbone of our American judicial system." It has the widest variety of work.

The supreme court deals with such cases as:

1. Breach of contract

2. Murder

3. Settling accident disputes as to who was the guilty party.

4. Awarding money settlements to people involved in airplane, automobile, and other types of accidents where negligence was involved.

5. Serving injunctions or court decisions that order a striking union to return to work and begin bargaining for a fair contract between labor and management.

6. Awarding annulments (a declaration that a marriage was not valid) after a proper hearing of parties involved.

7. Issuing separation papers to a husband or wife seeking to leave his/her spouse.

8. Issuing divorce papers to spouses seeking to live separately.

9. Issuing writs of *habeas corpus* (a court warrant that orders the bringing of a detained person to be brought before the Court). These are issued when a lawyer representing a client believes his/her client is being held in jail improperly.

10. Processing naturalization papers and approves them. People seeking to become citizens of our country have

to file naturalization papers and appear before the Supreme Court Judge to determine if (s)he condones making the applicant a citizen. The citizen then takes the oath of citizenship read to him/her by the Supreme Court Judge.

Elected for a term of seven years, each judge has a law clerk and other office staff for him/her to carry out his many duties. (S)he must make very important decisions every day. The judge needs to have much patience, be a good listener and do much reading and writing . (S)he must know the laws of the land and be able to interpret them to the people that come to his/her court. Also (s)he explains to the jury the cases (s)he hears and the sentences (s)he gives to those found guilty by the jury. The supreme court judge has a magnitude of power which (s)he exercises with wisdom and deliberation.

The County Court

The County court, like the supreme court, has UNLIMITED JURISDICTION over all criminal cases in which the grand jury has found an indictment (charge, accusation). This includes youthful offender cases, 99% of which are criminal in nature.

Judges are elected for a term of ten years. County court judges must be the kind of person that can deal with difficult cases. A lot of emotion is expressed during a murder trial and the judge has court officers that help maintain order in the court. A murder trial where either the victim, or the defendant, is a well-known figure will attract many media persons, who will want to write stories about the trial and people involved in it. Witnesses, defense lawyers, and prosecuting attorneys are constantly sought for interviews for comments about the trial.

The judge must constantly remind the jury about not to discuss the trial with anyone from the media, family, or friends. If someone does discuss what is going on in the courtroom with another person, that person could express that information to the media and see it spread all over the community. In this case, the judge is concerned about the possibility of a mistrial.

Judges must be knowledgeable about the law relating to criminal trials and know court procedure to explain to the jury their responsibility in criminal trials. (S)he may require the jury to be SEQUESTERED (held isolated or secluded) until a decision is made. Members of the jury are not happy about such a judicial decision, but realize that it may be necessary in order to bring in a fair verdict.

The County court judge has an office staff, including a law clerk, who assists with research in the law books. The law clerk is a graduate of law school, and can practice law, but chooses to work with a judge on court proceedings. Other office workers in addition help the judge carry out the heavy responsibilities the job requires.

Commissioner of Jurors

Fifty-two weeks of every year, selected citizens across our land receive a SUMMONS to serve as a trial juror. These citizens are needed in our court system to provide the opportunity for an accused person to be tried in court, where a PROSECUTOR presents evidence to prove whether the (s)he is guilty of the wrong (s)he is accused of doing. The accused is represented by a person called a DEFENSE ATTORNEY. The accused is called the DEFENDANT.

The commissioner of jurors has the responsibility of sending out summonses to citizens needed to hear evidence presented by the PROSECUTOR and DEFENSE ATTORNEY to decide guilt or innocence of the person accused. Jury trials are an important part of the judicial branch of government.

It is a duty not always welcomed by the person receiving the summons. It takes the person away from his/her job and does not pay very much ($15 per day, plus travel expenses). Also, many do not like being put in the position of having to state whether a person is guilty of a crime (like murder) which will sentence a person to spend the rest of his/her life behind bars. In the past twenty years the commissioner of jurors has experienced difficulty in finding enough jurors to serve.

The commissioner of jurors holds an APPOINTED position, which carries out the following duties:

1. Sending out summonses to prospective jurors so that they may serve on:

    a. **Civil Trials** (between two citizens, corporations, etc.). Usually the jury on a civil trial consists of SIX jurors and one alternate (someone who replaces a juror if one of the six needs to leave because of illness or other serious reasons). A civil trial is decided by a majority decision of at least four to two. The person who sues the other person is called the PLAINTIFF. The person who is being sued is called the defendant. Lawyers usually represent both the plaintiff and the defendant.

b. **Criminal trials** (where a person is accused by the district attorney of having committed a serious crime called a felony). Criminal trials consist of TWELVE jurors and two alternates. The first person to be picked for the jury is usually appointed as the FOREPERSON of the jury. Decisions have to be unanimous in criminal cases. Even if one person disagrees on the VERDICT (decision), a HUNG JURY is announced. The judge declares a mistrial and a new trial has to be arranged. Most jury trials usually end in a verdict of either "guilty" or "not guilty."

2. Sending out summonses to prospective jurors to serve on a **GRAND JURY**. Not many citizens serve on a grand jury. This kind of jury has the responsibility of being available to appear before the district attorney to hear evidence presented by the district attorney about a criminal case (s)he would like to bring to trial. Once the district attorney presents the evidence to the grand jury, they deliberate (talk it over with each other), coming to a decision whether there is sufficient evidence for the district attorney to go before a judge and ask that the accused be INDICTED (charged with the crime).

Then begin the proceedings for a criminal trial, where the accused are given the opportunity to seek an attorney. The district attorney prepares to present his/her case to the jury. If the grand jury believes that the district attorney has not presented enough evidence, they can tell him/her that no trial should be held. The accused is then discharged from the jurisdiction of the courts and can return to his/her normal way of life.

As you can see, by making the decision whether someone needs to defend his/her innocence in front of a judge and jury, the grand jury has a considerable responsibility to the people. A district attorney recognizes this important fact and is therefore careful not to bring charges against a person before the grand jury unless (s)he has an "AIR-TIGHT CASE!"

A grand jury serves for a period of time (one month) and is then released from their responsibility until called again in a few years. A grand jury consists of twenty-four jurors. Civil and criminal jurors are usually kept for a period of about two weeks. If they are EMPANELLED (selected to serve on a jury), they will need to serve until the trial is over. Most trials usually average about two weeks.

How Does a Person Get a Summons to Serve as a Juror?

Many citizens believe that a juror is selected from those who vote during elections or are registered voters. This is not the only way jurors are called upon to serve, but this may be one of the reasons why many citizens don't vote. If you have a driver's license you are a possible candidate to be called to serve on the jury. Usually the commissioner of jurors is very fair to those who seek to be excused. Sometimes the commissioner will postpone your time of service to another part of the year. In recent times, less and less prospective jurors have been excused.

Is Every Trial (Civil, Criminal) Tried Before a Jury?

NO! An accused person can request that the case be tried before a judge and accept the judge's decision after (s)he hears all the evidence. The trial is conducted in the same manner except that the decision is made by the judge. In a civil trial, both parties have to agree to not having a trial by jury. In a criminal trial only the defendant needs to request a trial without a jury.

What Happens When You Report For Jury Duty?

Usually a prospective juror is asked to report to the central jury room on a Monday morning at around 9:00 A.M. The central jury room contains over 200 seats that are not very comfortable. A prospective juror usually brings enough reading material to keep occupied until his/her name is called to be considered for impanelment.

At about 10:00 A.M., a jury clerk will start calling out names to make sure that all who received a summons is present. If a person fails to answer to his/her name, that person could face a CONTEMPT OF COURT charge. This may mean incurring a stiff fine, or being brought to trial and sent to jail for thirty days. Usually, the person may arrive late and be warned not to be tardy the next time.

After the roll call has been completed, the commissioner of jurors appears before, and welcomes the jurors. The jurors are shown a video stressing what it means to serve on a jury and the importance of a jury system in our democracy. The film lasts about fifteen minutes.

At about 11:00 A.M., another jury clerk asks everyone for their attention. (S)he is carrying a small barrel-shaped container which holds the names of all the jurors in attendance that morning. Cards are drawn from the container and names are called out. Those called line up in front of the person calling out the names. Shortly, a line of 30 or more jurors is waiting to hear what comes next.

The clerk then turns the jurors over to a court officer who brings the jurors to a room that contains chairs on two sides of a room, with desks and chairs in between the two sets of seats in the room. This is called the IMPANELLING ROOM. In this room, prospective jurors are interviewed to determine whether they should be on a jury.

In a civil case, requiring only six jurors and two alternates, the plaintiff's lawyer and the defendant's lawyer are present to interview the prospective jurors for the civil suit that will be tried in the courtroom.

The container with the 30 names is now used again to start picking the jury. Juror number one is called and asked to sit on the other side of the room where a similar set of seats is situated. Then jurors two, three, and following are called until the necessary jurors are now seated in the jury side of the room. Those not called remain in their seats.

At this point, each lawyer starts asking the selected jurors questions. This is done so they can get acquainted with the background of the selected jurors and make a decision as to whether they feel comfortable with that person to serve on the jury. Lawyers use a lot of intuition ("gut feelings") about prospective jurors as to how the juror will weigh the evidence and whether they are capable of being fair.

Both lawyers have the right to excuse any juror that has been selected. A juror should not feel badly about being excused. If any of the original jurors have been excused, those who had remained in their original seats may be drawn from the barrel-shaped container, replacing those excused jurors. The same procedure continues to take place until the six jurors and two alternates are selected.

At this point, those prospective jurors not selected are excused and can return to the central jury room. There they wait until called again from the barrel shaped container. If lunch-time arrives when they are dismissed from the impanelling room, they are released to go out and have lunch. They are usually given about one and one half to two hours to eat and are asked to return by about 2:00 P.M.

What happens to those that were selected for the civil case?

Those who were selected are brought into the courtroom and are seated in the jury box. The judge enters the courtroom and introduces himself/herself to those in the courtroom. The judge then asks the jurors to raise their right hand and swear they will execute their duty as jurors to the best of their ability. It is a solemn occasion.

Every juror realizes (s)he has accepted an important responsibility of listening carefully to evidence being presented by both attorneys and then making a thoughtful and meaningful decision that will positively or negatively effect the lives of those involved in the trial.

The same procedure takes place in a criminal trial as in a civil trial. Names are drawn from the barrel-shaped container. Jurors are brought to an impanelling room. The attorney from the district attorney's office, the prosecutor, and the defense attorney interview those jurors selected from the container and try to make a decision as to which of the jurors called will make an effective juror.

In criminal trials, much is at stake and it takes much longer to pick the twelve jurors and two alternates. More people are excused by the prosecutor and defense attorney, and the juror himself/herself may ask to be excused. You cannot be forced to be a juror in a trial of which you would rather not be a part.

After you have been selected to be a juror in a criminal trial, you are brought into the courtroom and the same procedure takes place. You are sworn in and the judge reads you what your responsibilities are in the case being presented. You also get to meet the defendant in the trial. It is an emotion-packed moment. You realize, as a juror for the first time that the person looking at you from across the room stands accused of a crime that may send him/her to prison for a long period of time and the decision rests upon your shoulders and those of eleven others. It can be awesome!

You are told by the judge that you cannot talk about the case you are hearing, not even to your fellow jurors. Those who serve on juries take their responsibility very seriously and follow the judge's order with great respect for his/her position.

IMPORTANT-READ BACK OF THIS SUMMONS
DO NOT DESTROY BRING IT WITH YOU
WHEN REPORTING FOR JURY DUTY

TRIAL JUROR SUMMONS

NO.__________

YOU ARE HEREBY SUMMONED TO SERVE AS A TRIAL JUROR at the Trial Term of the District Court of Suffolk designated to be held in and for the County of Suffolk

REPORT at 9:30 a.m. in the Central Jury Room, Veteran's Memorial Highway, Hauppauge, N.Y. 11787

Dated__________________

IMPORTANT— READ BACK OF THIS SUMMONS, PENALTY FOR NON ATTENDANCE

Albert J. Cavagnaro
Commissioner of Jurors
for Suffolk County

IMPORTANT-READ BACK OF THIS SUMMONS
DO NOT DESTROY BRING IT WITH YOU
WHEN REPORTING FOR JURY DUTY

TRIAL JUROR SUMMONS

NO.__________

YOU ARE HEREBY SUMMONED TO SERVE AS A TRIAL JUROR at the Trial Term of the District Court of Suffolk designated to be held in and for the County of Suffolk

REPORT at 9:30 a.m. in the Central Jury Room, Veteran's Memorial Highway, Hauppauge, N.Y. 11787

Dated__________________

IMPORTANT— READ BACK OF THIS SUMMONS, PENALTY FOR NON ATTENDANCE

Albert J. Cavagnaro
Commissioner of Jurors
for Suffolk County

JUROR WILL SIGN HERE

Fill in whether or not applying to be excused

Signature of Juror ....

Residence ....

Business Address ....

Name of Firm
or Corporation ....

Do not destroy or disregard this TRIAL JUROR SUMMONS as each bears a serial number for which we must account. Under the Penal Law a person who wilfully fails to obey this SUMMONS may be found guilty of Contempt of Court.

A check for jury fees and transportation expense will be mailed to your residence address by the Department of Audit & Control of Suffolk County, at the end of the Court Term.

REPORT PURSUANT TO SECTION 678-a JUDICIARY LAW

To be filled in if Juror is excused from service

Reasons Service postponed to ....

Illness .... Business ....

Other cause ....

COMMISSIONER'S
Signature
or Initials ....

ADDRESS ALL COMMUNICATIONS TO:

COMMISSIONER OF JURORS
Veteran's Memorial Hwy.
Hauppauge, N.Y. 11787

JUROR WILL SIGN HERE

Fill in whether or not applying to be excused

Signature of Juror ....

Residence ....

Business Address ....

Name of Firm
or Corporation ....

Do not destroy or disregard this TRIAL JUROR SUMMONS as each bears a serial number for which we must account. Under the Penal Law a person who wilfully fails to obey this SUMMONS may be found guilty of Contempt of Court.

A check for jury fees and transportation expense will be mailed to your residence address by the Department of Audit & Control of Suffolk County, at the end of the Court Term.

REPORT PURSUANT TO SECTION 678-a JUDICIARY LAW

To be filled in if Juror is excused from service

Reasons Service postponed to ....

Illness .... Business ....

Other cause ....

COMMISSIONER'S
Signature
or Initials ....

ADDRESS ALL COMMUNICATIONS TO:

COMMISSIONER OF JURORS
Veteran's Memorial Hwy.
Hauppauge, N.Y. 11787

REPORT PURSUANT TO SECTION 678, JUDICIARY LAW

To be filled in if Juror is excused from service

Reason: Service Postponed to ....

Illness .... Business ....

Other cause ....

(Judicial Signature or Initials) ....

A person dwelling or lodging or having or maintaining a dwelling or lodging in a county for the time between October first and June thirtieth next thereafter, is a resident of that county within the meaning of this section.

JUROR WILL SIGN HERE

Deliver to Clerk of Court

Fill in whether or not applying to be excused

Signature of Juror ....

Residence ....

Business Address ....

Name of Firm or Corporation ....

Do not make application to the Commissioner of Jurors or the District Attorney with reference to this summons.

The Judge alone has the power to excuse a juror, or to postpone service.

EXCUSES WILL BE HEARD ONLY ON THE RETURN DATE OF THIS SUMMONS

Wilful disobedience of this summons is a criminal contempt of court and is punishable by a fine of $250 or imprisonment not exceeding 30 days, or both.

A Grand Juror usually is not qualified to serve again for a period of two (2) years.

A fee of $8.00 for each day's necessary attendance plus mileage will be mailed to Juror by the Suffolk County Treasurer. Inquiries regarding payment should be addressed to Commissioner of Jurors, Riverhead, N.Y. Telephone ~~727-4700 Ext. 401~~ 548-3185

COPY

IMPORTANT – READ BACK OF THIS SUMMONS
DO NOT DESTROY BRING IT WITH YOU
WHEN REPORTING FOR JURY DUTY

GRAND JUROR SUMMONS

NO. ____________

YOU ARE HEREBY SUMMONED TO SERVE AS A GRAND JUROR IN THE COUNTY COURT PART OF SUFFOLK COUNTY, AT THE CRIMINAL COURTS BUILDING, CENTER DR. SOUTH, RIVERHEAD, N.Y. 11901

REPORT AT AM ROOM

Dated ____________

Albert J. Carpignano

Commissioner of Jurors for Suffolk County

IMPORTANT — READ BACK OF THIS SUMMONS, PENALTY FOR NON-ATTENDANCE.

SCO NO. 5A (11/77)

COPY

The National Census and Its Effects on the Political Process

A census is a conscientious attempt by the federal government to count the number of persons living in the United States and its territories. It is taken every TEN years. The last census was taken in 1990. Those who are knowledgeable about census-taking know that much is involved in trying to count the number of persons living in a given area. It takes several months to go about trying to see how many persons live in the United States, state by state, city by city, town by town, and village by village.

Even at their very best, the census figures are subject to change, due to the number of births and deaths that have taken place during that period of time. Also, there are a number of persons who are on the move, for one reason or another, and wish to remain unidentified, either as runaways or illegal aliens. In addition, some citizens have no address to call their own; these are the homeless, whose numbers can only be estimated.

The census is taken every ten years to determine how the representatives in Congress are going to be divided among the fifty states. There are 435 representatives in Congress. When the census is completed, the 435 representatives are redivided among the fifty states according to how the changes in population took place during the past ten years.

For example, New York State did not lose much in population but states like Florida, Texas, and California gained a great deal in their respective state populations. Thus Florida,

Texas, and California had increases in the number of representatives sent to Congress from their state, while New York LOST representatives to Congress. So you can see population shifts effect how each state is represented in Congress.

The same thing holds true WITHIN the state. Some areas of the state LOSE population and some areas GAIN population. Thus representation in the state assembly and state senate has to be redistributed according to the results of the census figures. On the County level this also effects the boundaries of the County legislators that make up the County legislature.

During the 1980's, for example, my legislative district was known as the 6th Legislative District. Since the 1990 Census, my legislative district became the 4th Legislative District. My house is still in the same place but the boundary lines were changed, and now I have a different legislator representing me in the County legislature. There are still 18 legislators, but they now represent some citizens that were not in their (new) district before the census was taken.

In the year 2000, another census will be taken and the process will be repeated again. This may be one of the reasons why voters find it difficult to know who their representatives are in Congress, state assembly, state senate, County legislature, and town boards. It is a necessary undertaking to assure citizens that each is fairly represented in every existing legislature.

Although our population has increased significantly during the past thirty years, the number of representatives in Congress has remained the same: 435! This means that each representative has a much larger constituency to represent in Congress as our population increases. The average population that a member of Congress serves in his district is 500,000! That is a multitude of citizens. The pressures on today's representatives causes many of them to leave after serving five or six terms. It used to be that Congressmen served over twenty, and even thirty years before thinking of leaving that position.

The same thing holds true for senators. Although a senator doesn't have to be concerned with redistricting (because the state boundary lines do not change when the census is taken), the size of his constituency does change, and the demands made on him/her increase as the population in his/her state grow.

For example, California now has 51 million citizens within its borders. Thirty years ago it had less than 30 million. Imagine the work load of trying to serve twenty million-plus citizens that were not present twenty years ago. Thus, U.S. Senators are cutting down their length of service in the Senate. This has a plus side, because past history indicates that congressmen and senators can become too entrenched in their position of power, and become the tool of special interest groups, instead of the everyday citizens, who have little or no time to keep up with what is going on in Washington, state capitals, and county seats.

Living in a democracy requires informed, involved, and patient citizens. As the dawn of the 21st century looms, we need to re-dedicate ourselves to helping our young citizens to learn how the process works and to establish good foundations to build upon as they progress in their educational development.

SUMMARY OF SUGGESTED FIELD TRIPS TO GOVERNMENT OFFICES DURING THE SIXTH OR SEVENTH GRADE STUDY OF GOVERNMENT:

1. Village hall (interview mayor)

2. Town board meeting (include visit to several town departments—clerk, tax receiver, town planner)

3. Division of traffic safety

4. Zoning board of appeals

5. Small claims court (district court judge)

6. County board of elections

NOTE: Author is aware that teachers have some difficulty arranging field trips to visit important governmental departments. An integral part of the course outline is to have students have these kinds of experiences. It is suggested that during the sixth grade students have 5 to 7 classroom visits of governmental officials and at least three field trips and try to have five during that year. Students gain much insight from the guest visits to the class and to the locations of government operations. The author has been teaching this suggested course for the past four years and has had no difficulty getting persons to come to the class and arranging relevant field trips. The author strongly believes that without the classroom visits and relevant field trips the material becomes more abstract.

SUMMARY OF SUGGESTED CLASSROOM VISITS OF GOVERNMENT OFFICIALS DURING THE SIXTH OR SEVENTH GRADE STUDY OF GOVERNMENT:

1. School board member

2. Library director or trustee

3. Fire commissioner

4. School board member

5. Village planner

6. Town attorney

7. Commissioner of public safety

8. Town committee person

9. Director of town youth bureau

10. Town council member

NOTE: Teachers can select from this suggested list five guests, on a once a month basis. Teachers can prepare questions to be asked of the guest during his/her visit. Suggested list of questions to ask class guests are part of this book to help teacher make visits more stimulating to students.

Students should be also encouraged to write letters to invite the official to class. Students should be encouraged to write "thank you" letters, including comments about how they reacted to the visit. These writing experiences can become part of the notes taken during their study of how our political system works.

SUMMARY OF SUGGESTED CLASSROOM VISITS OF GOVERNMENT OFFICIALS DURING THE SEVENTH OR EIGHTH GRADE STUDY OF GOVERNMENT:

1. County attorney

2. County planner

3. Citizens' affairs investigator

4. Probations officer

5. Legal aid attorney

6. Soil and conservation representative

7. Cooperative extension representative

8. County legislator

9. Social worker

10. Health official

NOTE: Again, teachers can select from this suggested list five guests, on a once a month basis. Teachers can prepare questions to be asked of guest during his/her visit. Suggested list of questions to ask class guests are part of this book to help teacher make the visit more riveting to students.

list of questions to ask class guests are part of this book to help teacher make the visit more riveting to students.

Once again, students should be encouraged to write letters to invite the official to class. Students should be encouraged to write "thank you" letters and include comments about how they reacted to the visit. These writing experiences can become part of the notes taken during their study of how our political system functions.

SUMMARY OF SUGGESTED FIELD TRIPS TO GOVERNMENT OFFICES DURING THE SEVENTH OR EIGHTH GRADE STUDY OF GOVERNMENT:

1. County legislative meeting of a particular committee.

NOTE: There are a number of legislative committees that meet during the week. These meetings are part of the larger body of the legislature and are work related committees. Students can interact with members of the committee and get a close look at functions in the legislative branch of government.

2. Public works department (interview a member of the engineering staff)

3. Civil service department

4. Fire, rescue, and emergency department (interview a fire marshal)

5. Visit the central jury room where jurors are assembled to serve on juries.

6. Visit to a supreme court or County court trial.

7. Visit to sheriff's office and County jail (minimum security)

NOTE: Author has taken students to all of the above trips in the past three years and has found students to be very impressed and effected by experiencing these field trips. At least three of the above trips should be taken during the seventh or eighth grade and an attempt should be made to have five.

County Government Information

A. There are sixty-two counties in New York State.

B. Five Counties—Kings (Brooklyn), Richmond (Staten Island), The Bronx, New York (Manhattan), and Queens—are consolidated as New York City. They have a city form of government with an elected mayor and a city council. Each county is also governed by a borough president.

C. Eight Counties—Cayuga, Cortland, Franklin, Niagara, Orleans, Schuyler, Tioga, and Yates—have NO County executives in their County government.

D. Eleven Counties—Clinton, Genesee, Greene, Herkimer, Jefferson, Lewis, Oswego, Schenectady, Steuben, Sullivan, and Ulster—are governed by an APPOINTED County manager and/or administrator.

E. Eighteen Counties—Chenango, Columbia, Delaware, Essex, Fulton, Hamilton, Livingston, Madison, Montgomery, Ontario, Saratoga, Schoharie, Seneca, Saint Lawrence, Warren, Wayne, Washington, and Wyoming—are governed by a group called the board of supervisors. The board of supervisors is made up of town supervisors, who are also the chief executives of their respective townships.

F. Allegheny County is governed by a group called the board of legislators.

G. Otsego and Tompkins County are governed by a group called the board of representatives.

H. Seventeen Counties are governed by a County executive: Albany, Broome, Cattaraugus, Chautauqua, Chemung, Dutchess, Erie, Monroe, Nassau, Oneida, Onondaga, Orange, Putnam, Rensselaer, Rockland, Suffolk, and Westchester.

I. Thirty-one of the sixty-two Counties of New York State have an appointed official called a public defender.